Awakened

My Journey from Pain into Purpose

•

•

Awakened

My Journey from Pain into Purpose

•

Melinda A. Taylor

ACKNOWLEDGMENTS

First and foremost, I would like to thank God who is the anchor of my life. Without Him, the process of putting this book together would have never happened. It was only by the faith that I have in Him that I was able to do this. Thank you, my Lord and Savior, Jesus Christ.

I dedicate this book in memory of my parents, Nazree and Mabel Taylor, who helped groom my writing process.

I acknowledge my daughter, Dynesha — you are a precious gift from God, and I love you for being who you are. I thank you for being there throughout the journey. I will always have a place for you in my heart, and my grandchildren, Nyla and Noah, Nina (Grandma) will forever love you.

I want to acknowledge my sister-friend, Sharon Lockett, the prayer warrior that you are. Thank you for always being there with your encouraging words to push me through to write this book. You were there when I was weary or distracted and wanted to give up. I thank you for the never-ending support that you showed me and have given me over the years. I will be grateful for this divine connection set up by God.

I want to acknowledge Pastor Curtis Norton and Pastor Tina Norton, for being my pillars in the midst of the darkness. I thank you for being the man and woman of God that you are. I also thank my Word Alive Christian Center family.

My appreciation to Pastor James Kuykendall and Elder Kathy Kuykendall, I thank you for your teachings on prayer, which showed me how to stand on God's word when no one else was there. Thank you for believing in me when I did not believe in myself; I want to thank the Agape Christian Ministries family. When I came through the doors from the trials of life, it was this church family who was there to embrace me with their love.

I would like to acknowledge my professor, Bishop Ahmed Screven and his wife Pastor Sabrina Screven, for imputing their knowledge and wisdom upon me and keeping me accountable to the task that was at hand.

I also want to acknowledge Pastor Ted Winsley and Pastor Dawn Winsley and The Family Church. Dynamic spiritual leaders who are making a change in South Jersey one day at a time. I thank you for your tenacity and consistency in conveying the word of God.

My appreciation to Beyond the Book Media and Staff for helping me to push this book forth. If it had not been for you, I might still be in the birthing position. I want to give a special appreciation to Chanel Martin, the founder of Beyond the Book Media, for standing on the mandate that God set before you. Thank you for your persistence in making Awakened: My Journey from Pain into Purpose be where it is today.

INTRODUCTION

In Awakened: My Journey from Pain into Purpose, I will show you how I've been awakened to the purpose and plan that God had destined for me by standing on His biblical principles. In this book, you will travel through the trials, tribulations, and challenges that tried to knock me down. My faith in God allowed me to overcome all that came my way, and I became the victor instead of the victim. This book is for all the single women — either a single parent or single after divorce or widowed — it is to let you know whatever adversities may come your way, God is your healer, He is your provider, He is your advocate, He is your comforter and so much more. Through your pain, God will show you how your past will become the blueprint for your future which is of His design.

Allow the Holy Spirit to awaken you then His Spirit will enter your soul, and you will become alive. You will feel different in a way you can't quite explain. Your life will seem brighter and clearer. He will open up and be made real to you, in a personal way and at a personal level.

You will understand by having a relationship with God how powerful He is and why He created you. You will begin to sense deep within what only you can naturally comprehend. I found through my journey there is so much more to life than what you can see, taste, smell, or feel. When you receive the Spirit of God, you will begin to fully understand the purpose and reason for your existence.

In your reading, you will see how God changed me. I finally came to a point in my life where I not only know who I am, but I know whose I am. I am now walking in the divine manifestation of God. You see, purpose and awakening go hand and hand when you come to know why you were put here on earth. The only way you will know this is by communion with God, your maker. As you hunger and thirst for more of God, He will give you just that, more of Him. God is the only one who truly knows what is best for you.

He is the only one who can mold and shape you. If you live your life accidentally, you will never find true fulfillment. God cares for you, and His plans for you are always good, never evil. You must believe what God said about you is true. He will guide you and awaken you to the way He sees things.

You, too, might have been like me – abused, emotionally and physically. You may feel like you have no value or self-worth. Saying things like, "God could never bring me back from this. I have done some things I am so ashamed of." God could take that stain out of your life and transform you into His marvelous light like he did me.

Now I will take you down the road that led me to who I am today. I hope that the Holy Spirit will also lead you through your adversities as you travel with me. I believe that you can overcome any challenge that may come your way and receive your victory with God.

TABLE OF CONTENTS

CHAPTER ONE

•

CHILDHOOD

I remember when my father said we were moving. I was used to living in a big city, lots of noise and sirens every day up and down the streets. We relocated to a small town in Bloomfield, New Jersey, about 20 miles from where I used to live in Newark. It was quiet there. You could hear the birds tweeting in the morning. The grass was neatly manicured around the suburban homes. It was a different lifestyle there than what I was used to. Being the only Afro American family in the area we dealt with racism on the block and in our schools. It was challenging at first, but after a couple of years, we overcame the challenges. We all became good neighbors looking out for one another. I understand why my parents moved from the busy streets of my old neighborhood. They wanted to give their children a better education and to live a better lifestyle, but in the beginning, it all came with a price.

My parents, two brothers, our dog, and I lived in the green house with white shutters. There was a green and white gated fence that surrounded our home. I can remember my mother making morning breakfast, and the aroma of the homemade biscuits smell under my nose. She had a country-style way of cooking., being from Alabama had a big part to do with it. There was nothing that she could not cook — her sweet potato pies and her pound cakes were the best. I did not pick up the skill of baking or even cooking from her. I can still hear her call me, "Linnnnnddda!!!" — from my upstairs bedroom – "come down here and help me cook this food." I would come down and start to cook something, then forget about what I started to cook. I knew my mother would take over, and she knew I was not coming back down. As well as being a good cook, my mom was also a very good seamstress. She could make anything from dresses to draperies. I remember her black singer sewing machine with a straight stitch only. She sewed many things with that sewing machine. I did pick up her sewing skills, and I, too, developed the skills of making dresses to draperies. It was a skill we had in the family. I do not know if my last name Taylor (tailor) had anything to do with it. There were also other aunts and cousins in my family who develop this skill too. Many of us find ourselves working very well with our hands in different capacities.

My mother and I had a complicated relationship, yet I learned many things from her but still, we did not get along. She was a very stern kind of woman — most women of her era were. They were a no-nonsense kind of people. As I am now an adult, I have come to find out you never know what's going on inside a person's past. My mother was private, never telling her children anything much about her past. She was one of eleven children, six brothers, and five sisters. I found out most of the things about my mother through my aunts and uncles. She appeared to be serious all the time. She seemed to be all about business – starched, never having fun. When she did laugh, she would straighten up as if to appear she is out of poise. The relationship my mom and I did have was as if I was an estranged child. It seemed to me that she was always out for her boys or my brothers, Stanley and Tyrone. They could do no wrong in her sight and I could do nothing right. As for mom and I, we were like oil and water, never agreeing on the same thing. This went on way into my adult life. So, what I did was always strive for the better. I would say to myself that I would prove to her that she was wrong. It was not until I became older and moved out on my own that our relationship became more stable.

My relationship with my dad was different from that of my mom. I believe me being his only daughter had a lot to do with it. Anything that I wanted, if my father could get it, it was mine. After all, I was the only girl in the family. He was a man who provided for his family in so many ways. He was a hard-working man, working two or three jobs. His jobs had many names — a seamstress, a mechanic, a landscaper, but to me, his mastery was in carpentry. I even remember him sewing the upholstery in his truck with the black Singer sewing machine. When you fast-forward that till today, he would do well on the DIY channel and shows like the Property Brothers, Fixer Upper, or Flipping Houses. I was always amazed by my dad, he only had a fifth-grade education, but the things he could do were miraculous. He was an architect in his own right. He could build a home from the bottom up. I watched him build our garage in the backyard from the ground up, as well as additions to our home. I remember asking him if there was anything he could not do.

I remember walking to the store with him, where he would always buy me Juicy Fruit gum. It was my favorite. Even as a young girl, I was always outside with my dad. If he was working on cars, I was right there with him. I believe that's why I'm a mechanic in my own right today. I know how to check all the fluids in my car. If I had to, I know how to change a tire. He taught me how to drive a stick shift. He said, "you never know if you're with someone who drives a stick, and something happens to them, and you don't know how to drive one." He taught me how to drive a 5 speed, manual 1970 Volkswagen. I remember in the school parking lot screeching the clutch as I was driving.

It seemed strange to me then, but now I am using everything he taught me to my advantage. My father did not know he was preparing me to be independent. He spoke into my life at an early age, to what would happen in my future.

One thing about my father is that everyone knew him in the neighborhood. He had such a kind heart, there was no one that he would not help. It was a shame after he retired,health issues came upon him. My father had gotten to a point in life he did not even know who I was. The crippling diseases of Alzheimer's and Dementia came to a point that they began to eat away at his mind.

My two brothers were both sportsmen. Stanley played baseball as a pitcher, and Tyrone played football very well, he was a quarterback. They did very well until they reached college and were introduced to women. Their focus was distracted from their school work to other activities, I believed they both could have gone to pros; they were just that good, but God had a different plan for them. I was a cheerleader in college. Now my granddaughter is a cheerleader. Cheerleaders today have competitions against one another. Years ago, I just cheered for the college basketball team, no flipping in the air for me.

I remember when I was younger, I was always in a corner somewhere reading a book. Until this very day, I still have a desire to read. I have hundreds of books in my office. I have them on my Kindle, Apple Books, or any other electronic device that may be around. I find myself now always reading books that edify my soul, but that was not always what I used to read. To tell the truth, Jackie Collins was one of my favorite authors. Her books excited me in so many ways, but thank God I have been delivered, from Jackie Collins.

My childhood may remind you of the television series Leave it to Beaver or The Huxtables. A little disagreement here and there but primarily everything looks like the typical American family. As we all know the enemy has to rear up his head and as I get older life becomes more complicated.

•

CHAPTER TWO

NEVER ALONE

As the twists and turns begin to surround me, God enlightens me on who He is in my life. Most of my friends now being in their late thirties seemed to have steady boy-friends or they may be married. I was not married, it started to be a concern for me. You know everyone wants someone in their life to love and at this point in my life, I was beginning to feel a little lonely. But, I learned in my journey to be careful what you ask for.

I thought to myself one day, what is it that constitutes being alone or lonely? Did I think because I was not married, I was alone? I had friends that were married and they laid next to their husbands every night screaming from the pain of loneliness. It was not until the Lord made me realize that I did not choose to be single, singleness chose me. I came into the world alone and I will die alone. The point is, now that I am alone, what am I going to do? The Webster Dictionary defines "alone" or "lonely" as being incomparable, unique, or exclusive of anyone or anything else." Being alone or lonely is a gift that came to teach us something. In 1 Corinthians 7:8 NKJV Paul says "For I wish that all men were even as I myself, but each one has his own gift from God, one in this manner and another that. But I say to the unmarried and to the widows. It is good for them if they remain even as I am, but if they cannot exercise self-control, let them marry. For it is better to marry than to burn with passion." When you're single you have more time to spend with God because there are zero distractions.

Your focus can be on Him and Him alone. With a husband, there is less focus on God and more focus on other things like your friends and family.

Throughout my travels, I have learned that being single is not for everyone and it can be difficult to adjust to. Many challenges will come your way and the only way to get through them is with the help of God.

As you go down the road of loneliness, Hebrews 13:5c NKJV says, "I will never leave you or forsake you." God will never abandon, desert, or strand you. Let us look at what it says in the word Gen 1:1-2 NKJV" In the beginning God created the heavens and the earth. The earth was without form and void and darkness was on the face of the deep." Meaning the earth was empty, dark or nothing. The Spirit of God was hovering over the face of the waters". The spirit here is God 's spirit and it suspends over the earth. Let us go to Genesis 2:7 NKJV we will see "the Lord God formed man from the dust of the ground and breathed into his nostrils the breath of life and man became a living being." When he breathed the breath of life into us this was also God's spirit. If this is so, His spirit has been with us since the beginning of time. We have never been alone.

One of my favorite scriptures in Jeremiah 1:4 -5 NKJV "the word of the Lord came to me saying: before I formed you in the womb, I knew you; before you were born, I sanctified you; I ordained you a prophet to the nations." This statement from the bible is so powerful. This scripture insinuates also that He knew us before the beginning of time. We didn't choose God but God chose us. He knew our parents before they knew they would have a child. No human is a mistake in God's eyes. It doesn't matter how you came into the world, whether you were the outcome of rape, or if you were adopted and never knew your birth parents. No one, and I mean no one, is a mistake in the eyes of God. We are never alone, and we were never intended to be alone. God has a purpose and a plan for each and every one of us and until His plan is fulfilled in our lives, He will be right there with you.

There are many scriptures in the bible where God let us know we are not alone. In Jeremiah 29:11– 13 NKJV "I know the thoughts that I think towards you says the Lord, thoughts of peace and not of evil, to give you a future and a hope. You will call upon me and go and pray to me and I will listen to you. You will seek me and find me, when you search for me with all your heart. I will be found by you, says the Lord."

In the bible, David, who was a man after God's own heart, was troubled and battled deep despair. He writes in the book of Psalms of his anguish, loneliness, fear of the enemy, and guilt. He struggled because of it. Psalm 42:5 NKJV says, "Why are you cast down, Oh my soul? Why are you disquieted within me? Hope in God, for I shall yet praise Him for the help of His countenance." Because of his honesty with his own weaknesses, it has given us hope today for those who struggle.

Also, when you look in Judges, there is a Prophet named Elijah, a powerful man of God who hid under a tree in a state of depression. He was discouraged, weary, and afraid. After great spiritual victories over the Prophets of Baal, he ran for his life far away from the threats of Jezebel. He ran into a cave and was isolated there to avoid what was going on outside. While Elijah was in the cave, he heard "a still small voice saying to him," what are you doing? A man of such great stature, why are you hiding? Why do you say you are alone? So, you see you are not the only one who feels the tension of loneliness.

In Genesis 32:22, "Jacob was left alone with a man who wrestled with him until the breaking of day. When He saw that He did not prevail against him, He touched the socket of Jacob's hip until it became out of joint as He wrestled with him. He said, "Let me go for the day breaks. But he said I will not let you go unless you bless me!" Jacob was alone while he wrestled with God until daybreak. I believe we all have times in our lives we have wrestled with loneliness. A time of despair of not knowing what to do or where to turn. But like Elijah, are we listening to the still small voice that God is whispering so gently in our ear, or are we caught up in the trials of life? We must know it is only in the still small voice we will find our answer.

If you are not rooted and grounded in the word of God and not tuned to His voice it is easy to get caught up in the distraction of life. Frustrations and afflictions can come our way that will move us from the plan God has for us.

Later in the journey, I lost my focus on God and one of the relationships I was involved in I became pregnant, now I am a single parent.

Later in life, I realized as God continued to guide me through the ebbs and flows of diversities, He brought new people into my life and cast other's out. He made me understand that the only people I needed to be around are the ones who are positive and who will provide me with strength. To the negative people who aren't depositing into your life, walk away from them and don't look back.

I find now as I am going through this journey of singleness with a child it is important to have different support groups to help me get through this season in my life. I used to hear people say it takes a village to raise a child. I learned how to develop a chain of people who can help me with my chores. Family, friends and church family are good people to help you.

Friends can be a big help with your baby-sitting needs. They will be able to encourage you spiritually and emotionally. Friends can be honest with you with no sugar coating added. I have friends who will tell me what I needed to hear as opposed to what I wanted to hear. They will speak the truth of the situation and hold me accountable.

You can get help from your family. I have learned a new way of identifying what family is. There is your biological family, sister, brother, mother and father. I can even go as far to say cousin, aunt and uncles. Some people do not get along with their biological families. But they may have developed a bond or a truce with people outside their natural family.

We can look at your church family and they will also be able to help with your needs. There are churches who have single ministries that are there to help you with your children. As I will mention later in the book, I will show you how churches I was involved with were a great help to me and my daughter. They helped emotionally and even financially in many ways as they imparted into my life.

Many challenges emotionally, financially and physically can take a lot out of you. I want to expound on a little about how emotionally you can become exhausted from the weight of the world on your shoulders. There are many times when I struggled with bouts of depression. There were days I would stay in the darkness of my room leaving my child to take care of herself. I was going through the motions of life pretending all was well. I knew I would be pushed to the edge if someone else said that I was strong. I was only strong because I was hanging on by the strength that God had me. I do not know how people get through life who do not have God in their life. If you do not have any spiritual guidance to help you along the way the enemy can easily come in to control you.

There are many ways you can get help financially. I received help from Catholic Charities, they helped me pay rent for my housing for one month. Welfare helped me with food stamps and other needs I had to take care of. I was on welfare for a total of three years before I found employment. This was something I did not depend on but used it to help me get from the situation I was in at that time. I continued looking for jobs and even took some classes to make me more marketable. I did what I had to do, to get where I needed it to be. I remember babysitting for a friend of mine. She had four kids I watched, for her between the ages of 10 months and four years old. I thought I could help my friend while she was helping me.

Also, we must take care of ourselves physically, we must eat right and exercise to stay the course because our family needs us.

I remember a family member telling me you do not have the makeup to be the father also to your child. I should concentrate on being her mother and do what I can do and what I can't do, I leave that to God. She said I must just trust the process. I can be the first to say I sometimes felt guilty and tried to play both mother and father roles. I was told there was no need for me to feel guilty because her father was not doing his part and he would pay the price for what he did not do.

I want to take a moment to say you are not in the storms of singleness by yourself. God has anointed you to raise your child and be single. He knows your circumstances and He has equipped you for the job. He gives you the grace to perform what He has called you to do. James 1:5 NKJVsays "if any of you lacks wisdom, let him ask of God, that gives to all men liberally, and without reproach, and it will be given to him". All you need to do is call on His name.

•

CHAPTER THREE

SOUL TIES

There's a place God wants us to go, that deep place where no one has been, the place that He can only touch. The area in your life when you cry out from the depths of your soul, and you are screaming from within, but no one hears.

I am talking about being involved in toxic relationships. When you are involved in this kind of relationship you begin to see yourself as damaged goods. You let people use and abuse you. You are always looking for people to validate you to what they want you to be. You have no respect for yourself, and you feel devalued, unappreciated, and worthless. This happens when you do not know who you are or whose you are. It is this kind of relationship that will lead you down a path of pain and agony.

Let me go back to the tender age of eight where I was molested. Too young to know what was going on, too scared to even scream. My body could not move because I was paralyzed in shock. I thought I could always trust in my family. They were someone I thought I would be able to talk to. I thought it was the strangers outside the family you had to worry about. I did not know if I should tell someone because I thought I would get in trouble if I did, and they would not believe me. What do you do? This is such a hard decision for a little girl to have to think about. Here I have just been sexually violated, and all I can think about is if I tell someone, I will get in trouble. I knew it was wrong. Why did I not fight him off? Why did I not do anything? I remember him telling me not to tell anyone because it was our little secret. I knew everything about this was wrong. Day after day, week after week, month after month, became years after years. I let this little secret stay dormant within me. I told no one.

I found every man I became involved with took a piece of my molester with them. This led me down the road to lust, sexual immorality, and pornography. I became involved in relationships where I became used and abused, emotionally and physically. I walked around with a mask on, pretending to be someone that I was not. Because of this unlawful entry it opened up doors to a life of promiscuity. My flesh proved itself to be an enemy of mine because it would not listen to me. My flesh did not care if I was broken, because it was too busy being the slave to the sin, I became bound to. I did not realize what I was doing, for it was the sin that was controlling me, that had me longing for attention.

I wore this mask for so long I knew when to put it on and when to take it off. The road to promiscuity left me in places I thought I would never be. There are many like me hiding behind the veil. We become tied to the person we need to be untied from. The inner depths of your soul begin to pull at you as you try to get untangled. The tie seems to get tighter and tighter. You cry in the middle of the night, but there's no one there to hear you. The soul ties had attached themselves to me, and things that I did not want to do that is what I found myself doing. Paul says it very well in Romans 7:15–20 NKJV"I do not understand what I do. For what I want to do I do not do, but what I hate, I do. If I do what I do not want to do I agree that the law is good. As it is; it is no longer myself who does it; but it is sin living in me. For I know that good itself does not dwell in me, that it is my sinful nature. I have the desire to do what is good, but I cannot carry it out. So, I do not do the good I want to do, but the evil I do not want to do I keep doing. Now if I do what I do not want to do, it is no longer I who do it but sin that dwells in me."

The knot or the sin became a part of my anatomy. My emotions were taking over in a way I did not know if I was coming or going. One day I feel one way; another day, I feel another. It was like my hormones were jumping all over the place. A simple thought came across my mind. The men I had given a piece of me, I had a piece of them, and I had a piece of whoever they had a piece of, and the list goes on and on. Now, I wondered why my emotions were all over the place; it was because the bed was crowded with all those I was with.

This promiscuity spirit haunted me everywhere I went. It was years of living this kind of life that left me empty and in despair, and I knew not where to turn. So, what did I do? The ties were taking over me and my soul continued to cry out? I continued to do what I was comfortable doing. This is for the women who lost all hope and you do what you know how to do.

Let me expound on what a soul tie is. A soul tie is an emotional connection you have after being intimate, usually engaging in sexual intercourse. In the Christian context the bible never mentions the term soul tie, but refers to it as "knitting of souls." There are godly soul ties and ungodly soul ties. The ones I am explaining in this context are ungodly soul ties.

We can form an ungodly attachment with any person, place or thing. ..." you are a slave to whatever controls you." 1 Corinthians 6:19-20. NJKV"Do you not know that your body is the temple of the Holy Ghost who is in you, who you have from God, and you are not your own? For you were bought at a price therefore, glorify God in your body and in your spirit, which are God's."

Evil spirits are able to enter when spiritual boundaries are violated. God has set boundaries that govern our relationships set by God for marriage. It is through soul ties a spiritual channel is formed. In a godly marriage the Holy Spirit flows between a husband

and his wife. The same principle holds in demonic soul ties. When there is the joining of two in an ungodly relationship through evil spirits one person opens up the other person for similar spirits. We must guard ourselves so we don't open our hearts to the wrong people. Jesus came to set us free, but our ungodly relationships take us captive. Once we know how the enemy enslaves us, we can resist the wiles of the devil. 1 Peter 5:8 (NKJV) "Be sober, be vigilant, because your adversary the devil walks about like a roaring lion, seeking whom he may devour."

We must know exactly what our soul, body and spirit represent. Our soul is that which perceives the psychological realm. Our soul is our personality; it is who we are. It is with our soul we think, reason, consider, and remember. We experience emotions like happiness, love, sorrow, anger, and compassion. We are able to choose and make decisions in our soulish realm. When your soul (mind, will and emotions) has been bound to toxic people. They have a way of manipulating and controlling you and this results in emotional and psychological addiction. When you're not married and form these relationships, the deeper the intimacy the deeper the bond, the stronger the cord, the more difficult the rope becomes twisted.

Our body is our external part. It is our world conscious. This is where we stay in contact with the material world. The body is visible. It is the part that goes back in the ground or back to the dust.

Your spirit-man is the part of you which is connected with God. It is the innermost source of your identity. In 1 Corinthians 2:10-12 (NLT) "it was to us that God revealed these things by His spirit. For his Spirit searches out everything and shows us God's deep secrets. No one can know a person's thoughts except that person's own spirit, and no one can know God's thoughts except

God's own Spirit. We have received God's Spirit so we can know the wonderful things God has freely given us".

When you live a spirit–filled life your inner man knows when someone is not of God. Because no one knows your thoughts like your spirit does. It is the spirit which searches out the deep things of God. The spirit knows God's will. The spirit man communicates with God about your spirit. There is no way that a spirit–filled man can be involved with a soul which is toxic. Because light does not mix with darkness. God says in the latter portion of 1 Peter 2:9 "he brings us out of darkness into His marvelous light".

In relationships, God would rather see you alone and broken hearted than soul tied and happy. Because a broken heart can and will heal over time, but an ungodly soul tie will eventually kill or ruin the lives of everyone that it is bound to. Have you ever heard on the news that a woman or a man killed her lover in a relationship? This is what an ungodly relationship can do. There are many toxic relationships, and I was a part of one. I should've died from it. If it had not been for the hands of God that was in my life I would not be here to write about my testimony.

I was living a life that was not pleasing to God. In God's eyes, it is a repeated violation of His standard for sex. God created sex as a beautiful expression of love that would propagate the species, but He also knows the devastation that results from abusing the gift. Promiscuity is an abuse of the power of sexuality. It robs those who practice it of the ability to understand true intimacy. It steals much of their self–worth, dignity, and purity of heart. We can easily see that promiscuity is the many problems of the world today.

Because of promiscuity the world is running rampant, it has brought on many social diseases such as abortions, STDs, AIDS, adultery, divorce, rape, and pornography. If people followed God's instructions about sex, many of these issues would not have come about.

God warned us about promiscuity in His word; it states that sexual immorality is a sin that separates us from God. I do believe that sexual molestation led me to live this kind of lifestyle. I believe it opened up doors of promiscuity in my life. But we can't let that be an excuse for us living that kind of lifestyle. God's word Galatians 5:19–21 NJKVsays, "Now the works the flesh are evident, which are adultery, fornication, uncleanness, lewdness, idolatry, sorcery, hatred, contentions, jealousies, outburst of wrath, selfish ambitions, dissensions, heresies, envy, murders, drunkenness, revelries, and the like of which I tell you beforehand, just as I also told you in time past, that those who practice such things will not inherit the kingdom of God." God's word says those who continue to violate themselves by having sexual relations with multiple people do not have a heart transformed by the power of the Holy Spirit.

Let me explain something to you. It does not matter what kind of woman you may be while you are in a toxic relationship. Some people think you have to have a low income, be on welfare, or be strung out on drugs to be in a toxic relationship. Some may view them as weak and immature, but people fail to understand that women can also be responsible or educated. There are a lot of housewives whose marriages are toxic and they feel they are trapped. Many women can be beautiful, smart, loving, and caring, and still be addicted to the pain of being soul tied to someone. It is not just any kind of pain that you are tied to. It is emotional pain from a toxic relationship. After you have experienced hurt, deceit, and sometimes abuse from a man you may love, you might find it difficult to let go or move on. Some people might say I would not have those problems because I would do this, or that if it was me. But you do not know until you are involved in this kind of relationship, and you begin to feel the pulls.

The signs you are involved in a toxic relationship is when you are living more in the past than in the present. You justify his bad actions and you say to yourself he really is a good guy. But that good guy seems to bring you more pain than joy. Not only is there emotional pain, but you begin to see the results of the physical pain also. Your values and your beliefs are different from each other, but you keep holding on and believing that things will get better.

Let me tell you something you must first love and respect yourself enough to walk away from anyone or anything that does not lead you to a closer relationship with God and help you grow mentally and spiritually.

The word says in 1 Corinthians 6:18 (NKJV) "flee from sexuality and morality. Every sin that a man does is outside the body, but he who commits sexual immorality sins against his own body."

Jesus paid the price for you. He redeemed you with His shed blood. Therefore, you are no longer a slave to sin. When you practice sexual immorality, you are delivering yourself to what Christ has delivered you from. The thief has no intention to pay the full price for your soul after all, he cannot afford you. Another way to say this is do not sell your soul to the devil it is not worth it. The only way he can reach you is for you to lower yourself to him. Because you were purchased by the precious blood of Jesus Christ, Satan cannot touch you. Since you are hidden underneath the wings of God and locked away in his heart, Satan cannot steal you. Jesus is not going to oppose your will, which means if you chose to go to Satan, he would let you go. You cannot say God made me do it because God will never tempt you beyond what you want to be tempted. It's best said in 1Corinthians 10:13, NKJV "No temptation has overtaken you except such as common to man but God is faithful who will allow you to be tempted beyond what you were able but with the temptation will also make the way of escape that you may be able to bear it." Any deviations from God's divisional plans for relationships are an abomination to God. When you have a covenant spiritually, it is defined as an agreement between God and man or between a married man and a woman. Having a sexual covenant is an agreement you have with the person you're having sex with. When a woman engages in sexual intercourse for the first time, the hymen tears, releasing blood flow.

Let me explain what a hymen is. If I would have known, I might not have gone down the path I did. The hymen is the delicate pinkish membrane that covers the vaginal opening in a woman's body. There is no biological function for the hymen, but it is more spiritual than physical. In her book Why the Hymen, Sheila Cooley explains the hymen is to seal the entrance to the vagina, a seal that serves as a mark of authentication or assurance and confirming authenticity. A seal that functions in securing an area to prevent unlawful passage, this blood flows over the male penis and onto the bed. The shedding of blood initiated by the breaking or cutting of the hymen is a covenant between a man and a woman. Your bodies are sacred. Your body belongs to God, just as I said earlier. You have been bought with a price. Blood has been shed on the cross for you.

In the Jewish culture, a man and a woman become officially husband and wife on their wedding night. It was through the act of sexual intercourse that a blood covenant was formed. This blood covenant, witnessed by God himself, sealed the two together as one in body, soul, and spirit. Due to the presence of blood on the wedding night, a special cloth would be placed underneath the couple as they engaged in sex for the first time. This cloth, also known as the women's token of virginity, would be kept in safekeeping with the bride's father — if her husband or anyone else ever accused her of not being a virgin on her wedding night. The blood cloth or tokens of virginity could be spread before the village elders as proof that the woman was a virgin.

In Matthew 19:5–6 NKJV it says, "For this reason a man shall leave his father and mother and be joined to his wife, and the two shall become one flesh? So then, they are no longer two, but one flesh. Therefore, what God has joined together, let no man separate."

As earlier soul ties will make you feel confused because you are outside the will of God, and you will have no peace. You will be miserable because you persist in doing something against God's will. There will be a misery that will not go away. Your mind will be tormented, and Satan will invade your soul. You will never be at rest. The most important thing you do not realize is that every person you have a sexual encounter with is tied to you.

Sex does more than eyes can see. You must be careful who and what you allow your soul to be tied to. Do you ever wonder what your soul looks like to God? The question you can ask yourself is who is living inside of you?

What does an Ungodly soul tie look like?

These are just a few things women say about the ungodly soul ties they are involved in.

- I am drained by this person. All I want to do is get out of this relationship.

- I am on pins and needles with anxiety or fear.

- He makes me feel like the problem is my fault.

- I avoid telling him if I meet someone else for lunch, coffee, etc.

I know the Bible says sex outside of marriage is wrong, but I just can't seem to give this person up.

What are the steps of breaking Ungodly Soul Ties?

- Actively pray and ask the Holy Spirit to reveal all the areas of spirit, flesh, and soul ties in your life.

- Allow your heart to break before the Lord as He reveals to you where you have created ungodly ties of any kind.

I remembered Word Alive Christians Ministries, a church I attended years ago. The pastor's wife had a program for the women in the church to take part in a Purity with Purpose Curriculum Course. Wow! The course was breathtaking. I am still not the same after partaking in this course, and it could have been more than twenty years ago. I remember we had a session where the women would just gather in a comfortable place around the room while worship music played softly. We prayed and waited for the Holy Spirit to minister to us about our past relationships and reveal to us the soul ties we had been involved in. We wrote the names on a cloth then we burned them in the fireplace. You see you must cut the sin down at the root and remember it no more.

Keys for Restoration

- You must confess before God each area in which you willingly made a negative soul tie.

- Admit to God you have sinned. Take responsibility for your sin.

- Forgive yourself and release yourself.

- Forgive the other person; you must forgive and release.

- Ask God through the power of the blood to deliver you from the negative effects and consequences of each soul tie.

- Vows, commitments and agreements are also known as binding the soul as in Numbers 30:2 "if a man vow a vow unto the Lord, or swear an oath to bind his soul with a bond. He shall not break his word he shall do according to all that proceeds out of his mouth". The concept of vows or commitments can also be a means to create a soul tie.

- If any gifts are given by the person that may be demonic. You may have had connection with the unholy relationship, such as rings, flowers, clothing that would be considered as a soul tie. These such things symbolize the ungodly relationship and can hold a soul tie in place. You must get rid of all things that will keep you attached.

- The right mate for you will PRAY for you not PREY on you.

- When it comes to the unmarried, if we do not do what the word says there is a price you have to pay. Always remember no sexual covenant is more powerful than the blood of Jesus. Through Jesus Christ, you have the victory over the devastation of any sexual assault.

Those who have been sexually molested there is a hotline number you can called in the back of the book. No one should have to go through this alone. There is always someone there to help you.

CHAPTER FOUR

•

ABUSED

Let's go back to the beginning, to one of the many relationships I found myself in. This one was the most toxic. I remember his name was Juan, in the beginning it was wonderful and blissful. We used to always meet at this particular restaurant, the food was very good. My favorite was the surf and turf or otherwise known as steak and lobster. The conversations we had were intriguing, and they were very intense. We used to talk for hours. At least until the manager would say we are about to close in fifteen minutes. After leaving the restaurant, we always liked to visit a nice little club down the street. The atmosphere there was warm and welcoming, the music was soothing. I always liked to hear the sounds of jazz. So, we continued our conversations from the restaurant to the jazz club. The people there were very friendly. We would all just bask, listening to the sound of the music that was tingling at our ears. Before you knew it, he was dropping me off at my door. It was such a beautiful evening.

This fantasy relationship continued for a couple of months before there was a quick turn. I started to notice signs of control when we were in New York City at the Underground Club. I remember it being very crowded there that particular Saturday. The Underground was three floors of dancing and entertainment. Everyone there was just having a good time. After a long work week, being there was refreshing. You were able to let your hair down. As we arrived at The Underground, I remember being dressed for the occasion. I remember he bought the dress I was wearing, and I was wearing it very well. The men were staring at me as I was passing by them at the club. Juan did not like the attention that I was getting from the other men. I said to myself, you are the one who bought the dress. This was the first sign of me seeing him being controlling. He wanted to leave immediately, but I did not want to go. I believe he had one too many drinks so we left the club, and I just went home.

These are signs you get when you are in relationships with people that should set off alarms. You can pay attention to the signs, or you can ignore them. At the time, I chose to ignore the signs and continue seeing him. Why do we, as women, always like the bad boys? I believe it is the excitement they make us feel. Nothing is boring with them, always an adventure. Now years have gone by, and I must say to myself it has been a roller coaster ride — a ride that I should've jumped off a long time ago.

At this point, Juan had become abusive, not so much physically but emotionally. He was beginning to fly off the handle from the least little thing. I could do no right in his eyes. He had tunnel vision. I felt like I was walking on eggshells talking to him. I was careful with my words because I did not want the bomb to go off. I found myself tiptoeing around him. I just said yes to everything to keep him quiet. When the relationship was good, it was good, but when it was bad, it was bad.

I remember one day we were yet again getting ready to go to the city. He said he wanted me to meet his friend. The friend was a female. I told him after a bad day I was not interested in meeting any of his friends, especially a woman, but he insisted that I go saying I would have a really good time. As we drove in the city through all the traffic on 42nd Street, we found a garage and went to park. I was still complaining all the way there about meeting this woman. As we walked up the street between the crowds, we stopped in front of the Radio City Music Hall, and I saw Diana Ross on a sign in lights. I was so excited. He said, this is the woman I wanted you to meet. All I can do is jump up and down, screaming with excitement. When we got into the theater, we walked right up to the front. I had the second –row aisle seat. I could not have been any closer. It was moments like these that would take over all the bad moments we had.

Now, after years of dating, this particular day was a very joyous one for me. I found out I was pregnant. This could have been a good thing or a bad thing. I had a very good pregnancy. I might've been sick twice in my third month. Our relationship seemed to be stronger since the pregnancy, but there were times he would still act out. I had a beautiful little girl inside of me. I knew it was a girl, we named her Dynesha. Sometimes you just have a knowing in your spirit. The three of us used to do many things together — go to the park, the beach, or just hang out with the family.

Juan had such a hold on me emotionally I thought I could not get away if I tried. As our daughter became older, he became more controlling. I remember having to get a restraining order on him. The restraining order was only a document stating he could not come within a certain range, and if he did, he could possibly go to jail. Well, you know he broke that restraining order, and if he didn't, I did. There just seemed to be such a pulling he had on me, and I did not know why.

I remember us getting an apartment living on the eleventh floor. My cousin and aunt lived on the same floor as I did. It was always nice to have family around knowing that he was so unpredictable.

There was a time when I was home talking to my girlfriend on the phone and Dynesha was in her room sleeping. When Juan came home this particular day, he was either drunk, high or on some kind of drug. He was very belligerent, yelling and screaming. I remember him tearing the phone cord out of the wall. He was mad because of something that happened on his job, so he came home and took it out on me. I remember taking Dynesha and going down the hall to my cousins. Because his behavior was so belligerent, I had to call the police. The way he was acting, I knew I had to leave because we would get into a fight. As I said earlier our relationship was more of an emotional abuse than physical but that still did not condone the relationship. Because emotional abuse is worse than physical abuse because the scars are from within. They are not seen vividly like bruises may appear with a physical abuse. The police came, and I stayed with my aunt and cousin. The relationship became unbearable. He started to make a scene and that is when I said that's enough.

When I look back over my relationship with my Juan. I sometimes asked myself how we get together? He was into drugs and I was not. We were the opposite of each other. When I think about what I loved about him, he loved me for me, so I thought. Because I wanted to be loved I dismissed everything he did to me to stay in the relationship. In the past, most of the relationships I had with other men I was just promiscuous, having fun, nothing really serious. I know it sounds crazy but because I did not have the confidence within myself, I let people treat me the way they wanted to. I was very shy and introverted. You have to love yourself first before you can invite anyone into a relationship. Loving yourself starts from within knowing what you want and knowing who you are. Our life is a journey and as you allow God to mold you and shape you it is only then you will change.

In my research there are many women who are going through domestic violence as I was. Here I will share with you the statistics around the country where women are being abused.

The Coker-Robb Cannon Family Lawyers stated in October 2020 statistically many women are involved in abusive relationships. Since COVID-19, there has been a surge in intimate partner violence incidents across the US and the world at large. A study from the University of Texas at Dallas stated domestic violence increased by 12.5%. Other cities in the United States have mirrored those statistics. In March 2020, there was a study in the city of Chicago where violence there received 389 calls per week on an average. By the first week of April, the number of average calls surged to around 549 per week. This increase in domestic violence is not unique to the United States. China's domestic violence calls in February 2020 to the police increased by 300% when compared to February the previous year. Non-profit organizations and government institutes have taken note of these issues. As states continued to collect domestic violence data, many experts saw more reports rising in domestic violence during the pandemic as stated earlier.

Those are the statistics worldwide but let me give you the statistics right here in New Jersey. The National Coalition Against Domestic Violence statistics states 35.80% of New Jersey women and 27.40% of New Jersey men experience intimate partner physical violence in 2021.

Understanding the Cycle of Abuse

- When abusers initiate a relationship with the victim it is known as the honeymoon phase. They attempt to draw the victim into the relationship by being exceptionally charming. They will shower them with affection. During this phase, the abuser attempts to create the perfect relationship. As the victim draws the victim in, they may also subtly engage in abusive behavior. The abuser will attempt to isolate the victim from their friends and family. Control plays a crucial role in an abusive relationship. The more isolated a person is, the less able to seek help.

- An abuser will try to justify the abuse during a phase called the escalation phase. They will try to get irritable over non-issues, such as household chores. The abuser becomes increasingly more emotionally and mentally abusive. They may try to isolate their partner financially and engage in behavior like gaslighting. This behavior isolates the victim. Once the abuser believes the victim is completely under their control, they will escalate to stage three. Physical abuse accompanies emotional abuse into stage three. This type of abuse can range from threats (punching the wall) to direct violence (slapping, choking, punching, etc.). Once the abuser commits a violent act, they often shift into the next phase.

- It is in the remorse phase the abuser attempts to re-establish control over the victim. Once the abusers feel insecure and in control, they will repeat what was done in the honeymoon phase.

This information is accurate and to the point. I am a product of these kinds of abuses. The toxic relationship I found myself involved in left me in a place of being very fearful. I could not go anywhere without having to keep looking over my shoulder to make sure he was not following me.

In domestic abuse, it is not just the person who is being abused that is being affected. The Presidential Task Force on Violence and The Family of the American Psychological Association found that a "child 's exposure to his father abusing his mother is the strongest risk factor for transmitting violent behavior from one generation to the next."

We must remember what the scriptures say about domestic abuse or any other abuse, as far as that matter. Psalm 11:5 NKJVsays, "He tests the righteous, but his soul hates the wicked and the one who loves violence."

I Corinthians 13:4–7 NKJV says, "Love suffers long and is kind; love does not envy; love does not parade itself, is not puffed up; does not behave rudely, does not seek its own, is not provoked, thinks no evil; does not rejoice iniquity, but rejoices in the truth; bears all things, believes all things hope all things endure all things." I know I am not the only one who has been in a toxic relationship. Women, you do not have to take the abuse you may be going through with your partner. At the end of this book, you will find hotline numbers that may help you.

•

CHAPTER FIVE

PERSECUTED

I remember my parents talking about how they wanted to sell their home and move to the southern part of New Jersey. For we now lived in a busy section of Jersey that was overpopulated and they wanted to move to a slower style of living. Also, they were tired of the stairs in their home and were looking for a ranch–style home with no stairs. There was a friend my parents knew at their church, Mt. Moriah Baptist Church. He mentioned this small community called Willingboro in South Jersey that he thought would be the perfect place for my parents to move. I, too, was looking for somewhere to live since I was living with my parents at the time. I remember one day my parents and I took a nice ride to South Jersey. It was about fifty miles from where we were living in Bloomfield. We went looking in the area of Willingboro where the man at my parent's church had told us about. The homes were well– manicured and were rancher–style – this was what my parents were looking for. As we went up and down the streets and rode through the town, my parents later decided it was the perfect place for them to retire.

Months later, my parents invested in a realtor in Bloomfield and before I knew it, the sign was on the front lawn of their home for sale. While my parents were waiting for someone to buy their house, I started looking for jobs in the Willingboro area in South Jersey. As I mentioned earlier, I was involved in an abusive relationship. So, I was looking to move also to a new area. After looking intently for a place to live and a job I so happened to have found a job first. I made the necessary arrangements and prepared for an interview. I returned to take the long drive back to Camden, a city in South Jersey to interview at a hospital called Cooper Medical Trauma Center. A couple of weeks after the interview, they called and said I had the position. I was so excited, but the only problem was I now had nowhere to live. I remember once again returning to South Jersey on the weekend looking for somewhere to live. As I said earlier, I wanted to move not too far from Willingboro where my parents would live. Eventually, I found an apartment in a town called Burlington. But the only thing I would be close to is my parent's but forty minutes from Camden where my job would be located. I took the apartment anyway and said I will figure everything else out later. Something will work itself out at the opportune time.

Just as the excitement about my new journey was about to take hold, my father was stricken sick and had a stroke. It left him paralyze on his whole left side and other challenges started to take place. I remember he was in therapy for years to regain his mobility. This threw a wrench in everything we all had planned. My parents had to take their house off the market, and our plan for them to move to South Jersey had to be done at another time. I was devastated because I thought we would all be together in our new home.

Now, I already had everything in place as far as my job and apartment was concerned. So, Dynesha and I proceeded to go to South Jersey by ourselves. I remember my family helped us make the big move. I also remember saying to my daughter it is now me and you against the world. She was four years old at the time. We were now going to be fifty miles away from family because we knew no one in our new town. But, the only thing good about it was I also was going to be fifty miles from being physically and emotionally abused. Juan knew nothing about the move even though he lived about fifteen minutes away from where my parents lived. I had learned what to say and not to say to him. I recall someone at my old job telling me later that he came up to the job looking for me. I told no one on my job where I was going as far as he knew we just disappeared. I knew he would never go and ask my parents because they would tell him nothing.

As I look back, I believe what happened to my father having the stroke and all—though it may seem a little hard to say—I think it all was ordained by God that I relocated. I believe it was mandated by Him for this new journey he was about to take us upon. You never know what God is going to do in your life and you do not know how He will do it. If it had not been for the man at my parent's church directing us to a place fifty miles away to a town called Willingboro, I believe I would not be living in South Jersey miles away Juan. It was good to know my father's healing had started to take place and I believe God's hand was on all of us.

Dynesha and I began to settle into our new place and we began meeting new friends. I became good friends with one of the moms in my daughter's class. These new friends of ours navigated us throughout the cities in South Jersey. We are still the best of friends now many years later.

One Sunday, as I looked out the window of my bedroom, I noticed a blue school bus picking up people in the development. One of the little girls getting on the bus was one of my Dynesha's friends. During the week I asked my neighbors where the school bus goes on Sunday's? They said they were going to a church called the Fountain of Life. In the next town over, it was a very large church; it seemed to have about a thousand members of all different nationalities. I have never been to a church of this magnitude. I was impressed and overwhelmed with their hospitality and the message was awesome. The next Sunday my daughter and I were on the bus going to church. I thought to myself this was a time I needed to get closer to God than ever before.

Now I am enjoying my job in a new area as a Radiologic Technologist. It was very exciting. I have worked in healthcare for about five years at this particular time. One thing we need to remember is our life is orchestrated by God. Let me tell you how I ended up working in the health field. After many attempts of working in jobs with no substance or no quality. My neighbor Mrs. Carter who lived around the corner from my childhood home must have been talking to my mother. Because when she saw me, she asked me if I was looking for a change in my career and I said yes. Mrs. Carter worked as a Nuclear Medicine Technologist at a nearby hospital. She told me there was a Radiological Technology school within the hospital and I should go fill out an application to maybe start school there. Since I was looking for a change, I did exactly what she told me. The school was only for two years and at that time I had no children so I could do it. Now, forty years later I am still working in the field.

When I decided to work in this line of work, I thought it would be perfect and I would always have a stable job. I thought since I was a single parent a job would never be anything I would have to worry about. It is kind of like job security. There are many different areas in healthcare you could work doing the work I did. You can work in a hospital setting, outpatient office, doctor's office or in any state where there are always jobs available. You can work 24 hours of the day if you want. I remember working, eight –hour, ten –hour, twelve –hours or sixteen –hour shifts. My new job was at a trauma center in the middle of a busy city. Most of our patients were stabbings, gunshots and drownings, especially in the summer, it kept me busy. We also took care of a lot of patients who were in accidents on the highways as well as other traumas. I remember always saying to myself, if I was ever in a bad accident bring me to Cooper Medical Trauma Center in Camden, New Jersey. I knew they would save your life, because their team of professionals were very good at what they did and it was good to be a part of that team. The trauma center reminded me of University Medical Center, a hospital I used to work in Newark, New Jersey. I was used to the busyness of working in that line of work. I believe it takes a special kind of person to work in this type of setting. The compassion that I have for people I thought was perfect for me. We were living in Burlington for about a year now and one night once again loneliness started gripping me. I don't know why but I started thinking of Juan again. When you have a soul tie with someone, it is a whisper in the middle of the night that speaks volumes in your ear. It does not matter how long it has been. It can be a week, month, a year or even five years. If you have not cut the spirit off from the root, it will always be trying to call your name. Before I knew it, I had given him a call and invited him in my new home.

Now we were at a restaurant once again, the three of us. Dynesha was excited to see her father. It had been a while since she'd last seen him. Everything was going well. We laughed, we played, we all were going out to events. We all seem to be just one big happy family. He ended up staying with me and he found a job. Slowly he started turning back to the person he was before. We as women are always trying to change a man to be what we want them to be. The thing is if you do not want to change, you can't change anyone. God is the only who can do the changing and he changes us from the inside out.

I remember my parent's coming to see Dynesha and I one day. They were very upset because I opened the door for destruction once again. I did not blame them at all. I did not argue with them on their judgment of him.

I had begun to let Juan use my car at times. He would take me to work when he was off and he would take Dynesha to the park or somewhere she might've wanted to go while I was at work.

One day he picked me up from work and then he wanted to go over and hang out with his friends. I did not mind because he did this several times before and would come home later in the night. However, this time he did not come back with the car. It became night and day again and still no car, I will call her oh his phone and I would get no answer. It was now time for me to go to work and there was no car in sight. I did not know if something happened to him — if there was an accident. He had never done anything like this before. I had to call out of work and I could not take my daughter to school. I was really upset that he would be so irresponsible. If I would have looked back over his track record, I would have known better. Now, I had to call my brother down to my place because when he did come back with my car, I knew it was not going to be good. I needed my brothers for support and did not want to get my parents involved.

We all stayed and waited and waited and waited for Juan to come back home with my car. It was three days later that he finally showed up. He had some other guys in my car and they all looked drugged up. I was so mad. I had to make other arrangements to get to work and to take my daughter to school. All I wanted him to do was to take all the things he had in my home and leave. If I would look back over my relationship, I would see I opened that door for destruction in my life, because he showed me signs in my past.

It has been about three weeks since he left my house. I heard a noise outside and when I looked out the window it was Juan. He wanted to know if I could give him a pair of pants he left at my house. I had a restraining order on him at this time. He started to yell more and more. I found the pants that he wanted and I rolled them up and put them through the mail slot on my door. Well, that made him really mad and he really started yelling. I had called the police as soon as I heard the noise out my window. Before I knew it, I heard a loud bang on my door—he had knocked down the door. I mean the whole frame around the door and the door itself. I lived on the second floor. He was running up the stairs and he grabbed my ankle, then I heard the cops pull up. Talk about an on−time God. He could not have been more on time. The situation could have turned out differently and I might not have been here to tell the story today. The cops came and put him in the car and took him to the police station. The thing I hated most about the whole situation was my daughter was there witnessing everything that was happening.

After that incident, I went running again, this time I just moved across town. Dynesha and I were going on this path. I still believe God had put us on it for a reason. The only thing I did not know was the reason for it. New Job, new apartment, new people, new surroundings here we come.

CHAPTER SIX

•

SUFFERING

I saw him glancing at me as I walked into the job. His name was Calvin. He said hello and I spoke back. At this time in my life, I did not want to get involved in another relationship, but this one seemed to be different, or at least I thought so. We gave each other small talk at the job. Since we were the only African Americans there, we had easy conversations. He was a little younger than I was, but then again, I was always told I looked younger for my age. Slowly, we began to take the conversation out of the job. We went out on our first date, and it was very nice. The first, second, and even third dates are always nice. It's the ones beyond that you have to worry about. I had such a physical attraction to this man. The first night I was with him, we just seemed to connect in a way that was just so irresistible to me. He became a good friend, and I also believe this was another soul tie I was attaching myself to. Calvin helped me with things around the apartment that I needed to be fixed. I did not have to worry about him being on drugs. He did not want anything poison in his body, he would say. He was a bodybuilder, and he was very careful of what he put inside his body. Being a personal trainer, he began to show me how to strengthen my body with weights and eat the right kind of foods.

Dynesha, being older now, did not like my new friend. She thought he was taking up a lot of her time with me, but that was not so. As my relationship started to grow with Calvin we became to know each other more. I believe this relationship was mainly based on an intimate level than anything else, but I hung around to see what would happen.

As I went to pick up my daughter from school one day, I saw this lady that looked familiar. She was picking up her sons. It had been a long time since I had seen her. I remembered her name was Mrs. Jones We became reacquainted with each of our families. She had a daycare in her home, she watched children of different age groups. This is what I was looking for in my daughter. The only stipulation was that she did not watch children on Sunday; that was her Sabbath day. This was a problem for me working in the health field. We can work seven days a week, twenty-four hours a day. We later agreed that she would watch Dynesha on all the days except Sunday. I had to make arrangements for the other days. As we became closer, she asked me what church I went to. I told her I remembered at my old apartment there was a blue school bus which came into the neighborhood, taking everyone to a church called Fountain of Life. Dynesha and I found ourselves on that bus a couple of Sundays out of the month. But since I'd moved, it had been a while since I had been to church. I remembered Mrs. Jones and I had met at Mt Moriah Baptist Church, the same church my parents attended. Our families all went there, so it was nice to run into her again about thirty years later.

She invited Dynesha and I to the church with her and her family. During the week, Calvin and I were still enjoying each other's company. The weekends he worked like I said earlier we can work at any time being in the health field.

When Sunday came, Dynesha and I went to church with Mrs. Jones and her family. As we were going to the church, named Word Alive Christians Center located in Mt Holly, New Jersey. I became a little perplexed because we were going into a warehouse. I had never been to a church in a warehouse before. It had always been a church building with a steeple on top. Where is Mrs. Jones taking my daughter and I? I told Dynesha to hold my hand and not to let go. As we continued everyone seemed to be friendly and welcoming. We sat down, and the music started to play. I heard Mrs. Jones tapping on the tambourines. It reminded me of my childhood church I used to go to when I was a child. I noticed every now and then some of the members were talking in a language I was not familiar with. I was beginning to think we had been invited to a cult because things seemed different than what I was used to in a church.

What language was this? I had never heard anyone say the things they were saying. I found out later that they were talking in tongues, another native language. This language was brought on by the Holy Spirit. I heard it said it will bring you closer to God.

When the pastor minister the word of God it was powerful. The message that came across had me wondering a bit because I was convicted when the service was over, I noticed I was feeling a little uncomfortable. My lifestyle did not meet up to anything he was preaching which was fornication and holiness. When I attended my old church, I would go out laying, playing, and drinking, and when I went to church that Sunday, I did not feel convicted like this church. What did this church have that the church I grew up in didn't, I wondered? Mrs. Jones once again invited us to go to the Tuesday night Bible study. I said yes but hesitantly.

Here again, we found ourselves back at the church where people were talking in this unknown language. When I went this time, I had a chance to meet everyone, including the spiritual leaders. I really enjoyed them. They were very genuine. I sensed that I could talk to them about anything. They were young but very understanding. Many children there were Dynesha's age, and she was enjoying herself, also. This became our church after several visits.

Now that I had joined the church, the relationship I had with Calvin was dissipating just a little. I was beginning to feel uncomfortable being with him since my lifestyle with him was contrary to the belief I was turning toward. But I was not letting him go too fast because he was taking care of other needs for me, not just the physical ones.

I was enjoying my newfound life when one day, as I was driving in town, I saw a man from afar who looked like Juan. I realized as I came closer, it was him. It had been about a year since I'd last seen him. I'd thought he moved back up to North Jersey where his family was from. When I saw him, I said to myself he must have decided to stay with the friends he had met here. Our eyes met and hesitantly I pulled the car over. I proceeded to talk with him but with caution because of our history together. Come to find out, he was staying not too far from where I was now living. He was staying with this girl he had met in town. As we were talking, I noticed he did not look very well. He had lost weight, and he looked very withdrawn. We did not talk long because I had an appointment I had to be at. We exchanged numbers, and I said we would connect at a later time. But I had no interest in being involved in a relationship with him ever again.

There was a different concern this time around. I felt sorry for him because I knew his family, and he was not raised in the manner in which he was looking. He went back to doing drugs, and it looked like they were taking effect on him. I remember him saying to me long ago when he was fifteen years old, there was a man who had hooked him onto heroin. It was the drug that started a path to other drugs that were taking over his life. It had such a stronghold on him even though he tried to break away, he could not. Just think someone came into his life at the age of fifteen who introduced him to drugs. Someone came into my life at the age of eight and took my innocence away. Both these occurrences turned our lives toward a downward path we should not have gone down.

There were times I would see Juan in town. I even invited him and his girlfriend over for dinner. Because of Dynesha I was trying to stay civil with him. One day, Juan called me and said he had to tell me something and it was urgent. I was concerned, and I wondered what he could possibly tell me. I waited intensely for his arrival at my apartment. Finally, I heard the knock on the door. It was him. We did a little small talk, and I asked him what was so important that he had to tell me. Then he dropped the bomb. He said he had HIV/AIDS, and I stood frozen, not knowing what to say. He said I needed to have myself checked. My first response was, when did you find out you were HIV positive? He told me it had been a couple of months ago since he'd found out. After he told me this disturbing news, he left, and I remember taking a shower, and that was the longest shower I had ever taken. I was scrubbing myself and crying and very distraught about what he just told me. I asked myself how could this happen? My daughter was about fourteen at this time, and I had to tell her that her father was sick because they had rekindled their relationship. I remember telling her that her father was HIV positive and she responded better than I expected her to. I did get tested, and I did not have HIV/AIDS. God's favor was upon my life. His grace and His mercy. Periodically we would still see Juan since he lived so close.

One day, I remember inviting Juan to the church I was attending. He came to church one Sunday and I was surprised to see him. I believed he was really trying to change his life around. He started to also come to our mid-week bible study. It is surprising when tribulations come your way it pushes you into the arms of God.

•

CHAPTER SEVEN

IN NEED

My life really turned around after I joined Word Alive Christian Center, not just for me but Dynesha also. I saw changes in her. I liked it because I did not have to pull her out of bed to go to church. She got up and was ready before me. I began to join different auxiliaries. I thought this made me more accountable. I started out in children's ministry teaching. I said to myself we were learning together and I studied and studied to prove myself knowledgeable for the lesson.

Since I gave my life back to God and started to work in the different areas of the church my life started to change. As time went by, if I was not working on my job, I was doing something in the church. I was there every Sunday and Tuesday and any other day if we had conferences. The pastor started to see qualities in me I would've never seen myself. I started being a part of the women's ministry, and I was in charge of the dance ministry. I was beginning to look at myself as really becoming the woman of God He was calling me to be. I would have never seen myself doing any of these things I was doing in the church.

I was beginning to enjoy my life then one day I went to work and they were downsizing and said I wasn't needed any longer. I was distraught. For goodness sake I had a child that was looking up to me, I was a single parent. My body was numb. I did not know what to do. I had rent to pay and food to put on the table. The warm tears went streaming down my face as I rode home.

God was given me some ridiculous favor as I was weathering the storms of life. He will place the right people before you at the right opportune time. I remember talking to my pastors about my situation. They were so understanding. They pointed me to some of the available resources in my town, for they lived in the same township I did. I also received warm comfort from the congregation. When I went to church the next Sunday, I remember the pastor calling Dynesha and I went up to the front of the church. I did not know why, but I went up reluctantly. He mentioned to the congregation that I had lost my job. He asked everyone to bless me with a benevolent offering. This is an offering serving a charitable or goodwill deed. When I tell you I was overwhelmed, even the children came and blessed me with what they had. When it was all totaled up, it came to about four hundred dollars. You have to understand my church was not a large congregation. God says in His word, in Genesis 22: 14 "He is Jehovah Jireh, your provider" you better believe it. He will make things happen in your life you would never have thought of. When I woke up that next morning, I would have never known going to church with five dollars in my pocket and coming home with four hundred would be possible. My God, what a mighty God we serve. It might not sound like a lot of money, but it sounds like one million dollars when you have nothing. God was showing up in my life in more ways than one.

Time had passed by and Dynesha and I were just hanging out watching television one evening. We heard a knock on the door, it was my pastor. I said to myself that it's very nice of them to stop by because I was not expecting them. All of a sudden, here they come with grocery bags from ShopRite. Once again, all I could do was cry because there was hardly any food in my cabinets. They filled my cabinets and refrigerator with all kinds of food — chicken, steak, and even some junk food for my daughter. God was showing me something in the midst of all of this. God uses other people to bless you in your life in unimaginable ways. I went to social services to see if I could get any assistance from them. I was able to get one month's rent paid with a voucher from Catholic Charities. I remember standing at the social services to apply for food stamps and welfare and I asked myself Lord, how did I get here? I was doing very well making pretty good money, and now I was on the welfare line getting food stamps. I would have never thought. Sometimes in life you think that everything is going well and it takes one calamity and it all can be gone.

As you look through the Bible, many women were in this same scenario I was. Look at Hagar in Genesis 16:11 NJKV "The angel of the Lord said behold you are with child, and you shall bear a son. You shall call his name Ishmael because the Lord has heard your affliction." In Genesis 16:13 NJKV says, "She called the name of the Lord who spoke to her. You-are-the-God-who-sees. She said "I also see Him, who sees me?" As you look up to God you should know in the midst of the storm, He is your El Roi, the God that sees.

Hagar fled from Abram and Sarai from the abuse and the pain. She was alone, in despair and scared, but God sees all. The angel of the Lord spoke to her, and He will speak to you also. Even though Ishmael was illegitimate and not the promised child, remember this, God is the God who sees all. He is omniscient. He knows it all. He is omnipotent. He is all-powerful, and He is omnipresent. He is everywhere. There is nowhere that He is not. He is and was and is to come. When you go through the valley, He is there. When you go to the mountains, He is there, also. Do not think you are in your situation alone because you are not. God said He will never leave you nor forsake you. He is your wheel in the middle of the wheel. There is nothing He will not do.

At this point, I had been sending out resumes all over, looking for jobs in my line of work, but it seemed like all the doors were closed. As I continued to seek God in my quiet time, I was convinced it had nothing to do with me not finding employment. I believe in this season of my life God was showing me that He is real. Because everywhere I sent a résumé, they said I was overqualified, or they had no openings. I definitely sensed the hand of God all over me at this time.

Once again, it was late in the evening, and I was getting ready to go to bed. I heard a noise outside my window. It sounded like a truck. I got up and looked out the window. All I could see was my car on the bed of a tow truck. Yes, they had come to repossess my car. This was another time that I experienced numbness that had taken over my body. It just seemed like I could not win. I was thinking, how am I going to be able to go on more interviews? One of the members at Word Alive Christian Center found out my car was repossessed. Words get around when you hear something like that. Sometimes it is good for people to hear your struggle because you can be blessed while you are in the struggle. Do not always be too quick to say I do not want anyone to know my business, because you might entertain an angel.

Even though all the calamity was happening around me, I was still giving my tithes and offerings to the church. This church had taught me the principles of tithing and offering. This is giving back ten percent of whatever your gross earnings are not your net to the Lord or the church. The monies are used for outreach ministries and the upkeep of the church. You may hear people say I am not giving the preacher my money. But if you knew the principles of tithing you could not afford not to pay your tithes. This is what I did even with my welfare check. I remember hearing from one pastor you can never out-give God. This is what I held onto throughout my storms. People would say, why are you still tithing? You do not even have enough money to take care of yourself. I learned how to invite God into my finances.

I obeyed what His promises said in the word. As I look at Luke 6:38, NKJV "Give, and it will be given to you. A good measure, pressed down, shaken together, and running over, will be poured into your lap. For with the measure you use, it will be measured to you." In my eyes, as I said earlier, I could not afford not to tithe, the true concept of tithing disciplined and structured me. I made God a partner in my struggle and realized if I stuck on the word of God, I could not fail. I knew the word was true, so I stood on His truths, and eventually, it set me free.

Remember a man at the church who heard my car was repossessed? He wanted to bless me. He said he had two cars and could not drive them both simultaneously. He said, you can drive the better car, and I will take the older one to get around in. Let me tell you when you walk in obedience to God's word, He will send people into your life to bless you in bountiful ways. Excuse me, I need to praise right here. My God!! Won't God do it!! Won't He do it!!

Where is "Calvin" I guess you say? He has been a big help in the relationship. If something needs repairing, he can fix the problem. I found him also hard to break away from but I learned my love for God was greater than my love for him.

After about three years with no job, God had proven himself faithful in my life. The only thing I found myself doing to keep afloat were some babysitting jobs.

I remember this one interview I had, and when I left the interview, I was more confused than when I went in. Have you ever had an experience, and you just knew God was in the room with you? The lady with whom I had the interview overlooked my resume. She said I was overqualified for the position. I still can hear it like she said it yesterday. I am going to show you around the building as if I will hire you for the position, but I will not hire you.

She said you need to step out into the deep and stop being afraid, God has so much more for you. Well, I said to myself, I need to put food on my table now. She said there is greater out there for you, but you have to reach up and catch it. Yes, the person who interviewed me was a Christian also. I believe I had to have that interview just to get the word of God for that time and hour of my life.

By this point, I was desperate, so I was applying for jobs anywhere. I applied for a job at JCPenney. I remember applying for a decorating consultant position. I enjoyed going to different people's homes, measuring for blinds, curtains, and draperies. It was a job I thought I would be able to do well. But because I had worked in the health field all my life, the challenge for me was when it came to money. I was not used to working on commission. When you work in the health field, you get paid if you come into work or not. I remember having a list of clients on file, but I did not know how to actually make it work for me. My stay at that job was short-lived. I was so desperately looking for a job that was in my comfort zone, and that was in the health field.

After about six months passed, a job at Robert Wood Johnson opened up for me in Hamilton, New Jersey. It was far for me to drive to go to work, but I would take anything at that point.

It looked like all was going well for me until one day I received a call from the hospital, it was Juan. When I answered the phone, I was startled and he said help me I am dying. I did not know what to say to him since he came back into our lives. He really was trying to turn his life around for the better. I remember he went to church and a couple bible studies with me on Sundays and Tuesday. When I got the call, it alarmed me because I was trying to help him all along. After I hung up the phone, I called his girlfriend, asking her what hospital he was in. She told me, then we went to go see him. When we got there the room was filled with family and friends.

The next day I was tired, but there was a pressing need to see him. I remember going into his room and he signaled me to sit next to him in the chair. He said he must tell me something, and he wanted me not to interrupt him as he talked. I sat and listened to what he had to say. In a short period, he gave me a whole kaleidoscope synopsis of his drug history. I really did not want to hear it, but he insisted that I did. He went on telling me how many times he came in of a drug overdose in the hospital I used to work at — Cooper Medical Center in Camden, New Jersey. I thank God I never was working in the emergency room when he came in overdosed. I do not know what I would have done but God sheltered me from seeing him like that. As he continued talking it seemed as though there was an apology, he thought I needed to hear. When he finished telling his story, I said I needed to tell him a story, also, about a man I knew named Jesus before I left that room. It did not matter what he did to me in the past or all the emotional and physical abuse I had endured. I remember God told me he was a soul, and you need to be there for him. I needed to know that Dynesha and I would see him again on the other side. I knew Jesus was doing a new thing in me, I made sure he repeated the sinner's prayer with me.

The next week I was at church rehearsal for a dance recital I was going to be directing. I received a call that Juan had died. I was so grateful I had the opportunity to have the conversation a couple of days prior with him. I remember telling my daughter at the funeral, I know that her father was not a good father, but she had to forgive him for all he did to her in her life. Forgiveness is not for the other person, it is for you. "Whenever you stand praying, forgive, if you have anything against anyone, so that your Father also who is in heaven may forgive you your trespasses" Mark 11:25 NKJV. Forgiveness is for you. I remember at the funeral I told my daughter the man in the coffin was only her father's body or the shell, but his spirit had gone on to be with Jesus.

As time went on and after I accepted the offer from Robert Wood Johnson, the blessings of God were following me. God had to first show me who he could be in my life and that he did. The road he's going to take me down this time He will show me who I am in his life.

There was a time in my life I did not know who I was. I had low self-esteem, and I did not believe in myself. I thought I could not do certain things. It was not until God started pulling the veil from my eyes, showing me who I was in His eyes. He said that if you know who I am then I will know who you are because I live inside of you.

The relationship with Calvin started to diminish. The more I looked within myself, the more God showed me who I was. I did not have to accept the least of things. Calvin was all right, laying and playing with me, but when I invited him to the church, he would not go to church with me. Now I know anyone who does not want to be a part of Jesus cannot be a part of me. I said to myself that I would pray for him. I will plant the seed, believing that someone else will come into his life and water it.

As God continued to show me how valuable I was to him, he showed me right back who He was to me. I was able to break the ties that were attached to my soul and ended that relationship. I only mention two of the many relationships I was involved in, but there were many more that I was tied to, but as I was getting closer to God, he was delivering me from all the ties which I so entangled myself in. There were so many situations in my life that God had delivered me from, but I have been learning the more I reach out to him, the closer he comes to me.

•

CHAPTER EIGHT

GRIEF

I remember mentioning earlier that my mother and I did not get along. We were pretty much like oil and water. There was a pain my mother went through that was so deep only God could touch it. It was not because I didn't love her. It was difficult to love her because she was hard to be reached. I remember after I moved to South Jersey, God put a different spin on our relationship. Whereas we did not get along when I was younger, we became the best of friends when I got older.

My mother had been very involved in my childhood church, Mt. Moriah Baptist, in Paterson, New Jersey. She was involved in a lot of the auxiliaries like I was at Word Alive Christian Center. She sang in the choir. She had a beautiful voice. She was very active. My father played a role in Mt. Moriah, also as a member of the trustee board. My father, with his many talents, fixed anything and everything that was broken in the church.

Just before I moved, my father had his first stroke, and later in the years, he began to have a lot of mini–strokes. This took a toll on the family because my mother could not take care of him by herself. My brothers had moved out of the house long before then. We did not want to, but since the care was becoming too much for my mother, we had to put my father in a convalescent center, which was one of the hardest things to do. He was such an active, caring man of God. It was hard to see him become so frail.

Now since my mother was alone in the family home, we began to have Bible study on the phone, talking about the different books of the Bible. We enjoyed our time in the Lord together and would be on the phone for hours. I could see how God was reconciling our relationship from having a relationship like oil and water, never agreeing on anything. The relationship seemed to become like the blossoming of a flower with a sweet fragrance.

Time had passed, I remember not going into work on this particular day when I received a call from my mother. Dynesha, also had off from school and she was home. My mother told me she was in the hospital and if I could meet her there. I am so glad that I did not go to work that day. I would have missed the call. At this time, cell phones were not as popular as they are now. We did not carry them around in our pockets. I would have had to actually get the call from someone, and they would have had to try to find me. Working in a hospital setting I could have been anywhere in the hospital. I did not have a job where I sat at my desk all day.

We hurried up the New Jersey Turnpike, a well-known expressway most people traveled. "My mother was at a hospital in the town not far from where she lived.

As we walked into the emergency department, it seemed to be a very busy night. Something I am so familiar with being around since I used to work at a trauma center. I can remember it would be so busy at times, we never had a chance to eat any food the entire shift. I saw my mother in the hallway on a stretcher where it seemed everyone else was lined up, also. This is what most hospitals do when the emergency rooms become filled up. They line the patients up in the hallway.

When I saw my mother, I could see fear all over her face. All I could think of was we started talking with each other again, and she never mentioned anything was wrong with her.

As I stated earlier, my mother was a very private person and never mentioned anything about her health. So, when I asked her what happened she told me to ask the doctor. I thought this to be strange because she should have known what was wrong with her. I found out later my mother had been spitting up blood for weeks and never told anyone. I know she probably did not want anyone to worry about her. But, my working in the health field and the knowledge I have with the doctor's I thought we might have been able to catch it earlier.

After looking for the doctor in the turmoil that was going on in the emergency room that night. I became very disappointed with the doctor. It was one of the nurses who pointed out to me who the doctor actually was. When I asked the doctor what was wrong with my mother, I remember him shouting across the nurse's counter, "I believe it is cancer. I have to run some more tests." Anyone in their right state of mind knows that is not the etiquette of a physician who works in a hospital. I know he was probably stressed because it was a very busy night, but you do not blurt something like that over the counter.

When my mother heard the word cancer, I could see it in her eyes. She instantly became more fearful. We stayed with my mother for hours until she obtained the results. It was not until the early hours of the morning the doctor came and said she had lung cancer.

This was yet another long journey I traveled. It was with my mother through this horrific disease. I was there for every test she had to go through. I was there for every doctor's appointment and every chemo treatment. There was nothing that she had to go through that I was not there with her. All I knew was that I would never let her go through this alone, and that is what I did.

A couple of years ago the Lord woke me up early in the morning, around two o'clock. I remember him telling me to get a pen and paper. This was not hard for me to find because I always kept a pen and paper on my nightstand. I get these early morning visitations, and I always wanted to be able to write what the Lord had to say to me. I could always hear God the best in the still of the night when there was no noise. So, I had the paper, and I remember writing as if God was guiding my hand. I was writing so fast it astonished me. After I finished writing, I read what I had written. It said to honor your mother and father, and that was it. I did not understand what the Lord was saying to me because I always respected my parents. But what I did not know was this was for later in life and not at that present moment. I kept it imprinted in my head over the years, and I never forgot that night. Since my mother was in the hospital and my father in a convalescent center recovering from strokes, immediately that night came back to me.

As time went by, I could see my mother's health failing. It is awful to see your mother becoming more and more weak before your eyes.

Now, there was a decision I had to make, and that was to move from South Jersey back to North Jersey, where my parents were from. My brothers both had their own homes and they were faraway. Stanley would come to help every other weekend even though he was in Connecticut. Tyrone had a business in Ohio that had crucial mandates and it was hard for him to get away. It was just easier for me to move since I was living the closest. Also, I was in an apartment with a lease from month to month. Even if I did have my own home, I probably would have still made the choice I did. Because I remembered the mandate I had on my life to honor my father and my mother, so that is what I would do no matter what.

At the job I was working at, I had already mentioned to them my mother had cancer. I let them know I had to change my status from full-time to part-time. They understood, and they accommodated me with the change. But as time went by my mother's health worsened, she lost her eyesight because the cancer had started to metastasize or spread to her brain. I had to quit my job. Yes, I can't believe I said that myself. There was no way I could work in South Jersey and take care of my mother in North Jersey.

As I made the transition, it was as if I was in a twilight zone. I just saw myself doing it. I do not know as I look back how I did it all. When I was moving, I just grabbed all I could and put it in my car. I took a couple of trips once again up and down the New Jersey Turnpike with my car packed from the move. The bigger items that I could not move, I just gave away. I remember giving away an expensive couch to my girlfriend's mother, who had a ministry for the needy. I now realized that at that time I was needy. I gave away televisions, wall units, and lots of other things. I did not have the money to even get a U-Haul. I was moving into my parent's home, which was already fully furnished. Yes, I could have sold everything, but at that time, everything was time-sensitive. It probably was that I was on autopilot doing what I had to do at that time. You know, do what you have to do when you gotta do it.

As I was going through all the new changes, the changes were not just for me, but my daughter was also going through changes. Being a single parent and my daughter was seventeen at this point, I also had duties as a mother. Dynesha graduated that year, and it was a tough year for her, also. She was gravitating more to her friends, which was dangerous as I was taking care of everyone in the family. It was not that she had terrible friends. It was that I had opened the door for the enemy to cause havoc in her life, and that was not a good thing.

I made a move, and I now lived in my mother's home, taking care of her. My mother was one out of eleven children, and one of her sisters from Alabama came to help me take care of my mother for a while, which was much-needed help.

As I was going over my bills one day, I just did not know how they were going to get paid. I made payment arrangements with the creditors, and they were very understanding.

This was a crazy time in my life. My mother was dying, and so was my father, both at the same time. My mother came to me one day when she knew I was going over my bills. She told me to go into the hall closet, look in the vault, and there was an envelope in there. My parents had this large fireproof vault they hid in the back of the closet to put their important papers in. They thought if the house caught on fire for any reason, the important papers would not be affected. I went to get the envelope out of the vault, and I opened it up. I saw nothing but money in it. I was wondering why she left so much money in the vault in the closet. But I figured it out my mother had just kept cashing her checks from my father and putting them in the vault. Because my father stayed in the Convalescent Center, you had to show you had no money for him to be accepted and to stay at the center. My mother put my parent's house in my oldest brother Stanley's name. My mother would cash all her checks, and stored it all in the vault in the closet. When I went to get the money, all I know is it was thousands. I just broke down and cried. The very money hidden in the back of the closet in a vault equaled the money that I had to pay out for my bills plus there was a little extra. What a mighty God we serve. We have to remember He orchestrated everything in our lives so we can get to the purpose He has planned for us. Weeks had passed by, and my aunt had to go back to Alabama. I enjoyed her help.

I enjoyed this alone time with my mother. She now had pretty silver hair, and she seemed to portray a glow or a radiance. I looked at the glow as being God's glory upon her. There also was a peace she had come to have. My mother knew the Lord, and it seemed as if she had a talk with him about her condition. It was as if she had no worries, and she knew her redeemer was drawing nigh.

We had a hospital bed set up in my parent's living room because she could not go up and down the stairs. Being in the living room was so convenient for her, and I just slept on the couch near her.

I remember so clearly as if it was yesterday. Early in the morning, around five a.m. I heard a knock on the door by someone with a heavy hand. I got up to see who was at the door. As I looked out, I saw no one. I opened the door, went outside, and still saw no one. I thought that was odd as heavy as the knock was, and I got up right away. Who could it have been? My mother asked who was knocking so hard at the door? I responded to her that I did not know who was at the door because I saw no one.

We laid back down for a little longer, then I got out of bed because my sleep was interrupted. I said to myself, I may as well just start making breakfast. Our day went on like it normally does until later in the evening. As my mother was sleeping, I remember hearing my mother gasping her last breath. It was so heart-wrenching. All I can remember is all the time, we did not get along. But at that last gasping moment, it was me alone with her as she transitioned from earth to heaven. The knock at the door that morning was death knocking at the door. That is a phrase I used to hear amongst my elders when I was young. It was God calling her home. Later in the day, I went to the Convalescent Center, where my dad was to see how he was doing.

•

CHAPTER NINE

HIS FAITHFULNESS

Being back home at the house I grew up in, it seemed a little strange. Where it used to be a house full of noise and enjoyment with my parents, my brothers, and two dogs, it was now just me. After all the changes in our lives, Dynesha became rebellious. She was now 17 and wanted to do the things she wanted to do. She did not want to move back to her grandparent's house with me. She wanted to stay in South Jersey. She moved to South Jersey when she was four years old and she wanted to stay there with her friends.

With all the spiritual teaching I received from Word Alive Christian Center, I was sanctified and filled with the Holy Ghost. I came to a place where I was not playing with the enemy. I went into spiritual warfare. I decreed, and I declared some things over her life. I knew how to plead the blood of Jesus, and that is what I did. I prayed to God to let nothing happen to my child but to cause a disturbance in her life and send her back home to me safe and sound. That is what I stood on, and I gave it all to the Lord.

While I was waiting for my daughter to come to her senses, I went back and forth seeing my father in the Convalescent Center. I remember one of the workers at the center saying, you are always here. But after my mother passed, I thought it was my obligation to always be there with him. Since my brothers were far away, I was the one to look after my dad. My uncles and aunts would come to see him when they could, but I was his daughter. If anyone should be there, I thought I should.

I remember going to see him this one particular day, and his eyes looked very weak. When I think back, we thought my father would pass before my mom. Because he had many strokes and in and out of the convalescent homes and hospitals. You never know which way life is going to go. I was there with my dad, his little girl standing by his side all the way through. My dad had gotten to the point where he could not speak because of all the strokes he had. So, as I was looking into his eyes, it seemed like he was trying to say something to me. It seemed like he knew my mother had transitioned. I went ahead and told him that she did pass, and it was okay for him to let go, and he could meet her in heaven.

Looking for a church home was now my priority since I moved. One thing I will remember about being in the house of the Lord: you should always have a spiritual covering. You should have a pastor and church family who will be there for you for any needs you may have. As spoken of earlier when I lost my job it was my church family that was there for me.

I was searching for a new church home that had the teachings I experienced at Word Alive Christian Center. In 1995, I remember the Women's Ministry going to Puerto Rico for a women's conference with another church called Agape Christian Ministries from Paterson, New Jersey. Is it not a coincidence that this church is only 30 minutes away from where I now live? When you look at Jeremiah 29:11 NIV "For I know the plans I have for you, declares the Lord, plans to prosper you and not to harm you, plans to give you hope and a future." I look at how His plan and future orchestrated this union together. Here in 2005 ten years later Agape Christian Ministries is now my new church home.

I remember like it was yesterday. It was February 2005. I walked through the doors of Agape Christian Ministries, looking for Jesus. Even though I was fired up from the teachings from Word Alive Christian Center, life itself has a way of throwing you a curveball, making you feel depressed and worn out. I had lost my daughter's father, my mother, and my father was now holding on to his life. Dynesha was staying more than fifty miles away with someone I did not approve of. I was living in my childhood home with no one but myself. I was lonely when I woke up and lonely when I laid down. I needed Jesus more than I ever needed him. I thank God for knowing Him like I did because that faith I held onto was the only thing to keep me going.

I must believe all that is happening is working together for my good. I refer to my present circumstances as the dry bones in Ezekiel. The Merriam–Webster dictionary defines" dry as exhausted of any liquid or free from water, drought or sparse." Now, let's define the meaning of water "replenish or refresh." Ezekiel 37: 11–14 (NIV) says it best, "Then He said to me son of man these bones are the whole house of Israel. They indeed say our bones are dry our hope is lost and we are cut off. Therefore, prophesy and say to them. Thus, says the Lord God "Behold, oh my people, I will open your graves and cause you to come up from your graves, and bring you into the land of Israel. Then you shall know that I am the Lord, when I have opened your graves, oh my people and brought you up from your graves. I will put my Spirit in you, and you shall live and I will place you in your own land. Then you shall know that I the Lord have spoken it and performed it says the Lord."

I relate my life at this time to the dry bones as being hopeless, losing my fight to live. I look at it as a long time being in the valley. But just like Ezekiel spoke to the dry bones, I learned to speak to my situation that my life would come together and everything that was broken shall be made whole.

We must look to the written word of God and see how it can speak to our present situation. Then you will begin to get the strength to continue on the journey or path that God has you on.

Agape Christian Ministries stood on the same foundation that the Word Alive Christian Center did. They believe there is only one God, and He created the heavens and the earth. This Godhead consists of the father (God), the Son (Jesus), and the Holy Spirit. It revolves around the life, death, and resurrection of Jesus. They believe God sent His son, Jesus, the Messiah, to save the world. They believe Jesus was crucified on the cross to offer the forgiveness of sins and was resurrected three days after his death before ascending to heaven. Jesus will return to earth again, known as the second coming.

I was warmly welcomed as I came through the doors. The church was lively, meaning the Spirit was alive, and the word was powerful. The church stood firmly on the word of God, and its anchor was in prayer. As the pastor taught in prayer, I remember him saying if there was ever a time when you were in dire need, and you can't get man, you had the power of prayer you can hold onto. God is awesome because He always knows what you need at the time you need it. Agape Christians Ministries is what I needed at that particular time in my life.

I had no problem joining the church. I have been blessed abundantly ever since I joined. After I sat a while listening to the word and letting it minister to me, I began to step out and join some auxiliaries in the church. The first area I joined was the bookstore since I like to read. I thought this was a good start. I was getting to know other members of the body. It was a good experience. The pastor and his wife were laities that were approachable. I know of some churches you have to go through so many people just to get to the pastor. No, not here at Agape. They wanted to get to know their members on a relational basis. As time went by, my prayer life was becoming even stronger. I began to know more scriptures as they pertain to different areas of my life. The more I became involved in different areas of the church, it seemed my prayer life started changing. The pastors started believing in me in things I did not believe in myself. As I was growing in the church, I knew that God had appointed me to be here.

I received a call from Dynesha about three months after she said she did not want to live with me. She wanted to know if she could come home. When you leave things to God, he will take care of them his way. I said to myself, thank you, Jesus, for sending my child home safely. Just like the prodigal son, I welcomed her home. I was just glad she was not harmed in any way.

One day I was taking Dynehsa to the airport to see her cousin in Alabama. I received a call from my uncle saying to come to the Convalescent Center but not to worry. I dropped my daughter off at the terminal. Anxiously I proceeded to the Convalescent Center where my father was, and, of course, I was thinking the worst. The news was just as I had expected. My father had transitioned on to be with the Lord. I was at peace now. I remember asking the Lord years ago if he could please take my dad. I thought he was in a state that no one should have been. He could not talk, and he was confined to the bed. I will not forget my dad. My parents died nine months within each other. I thought now they are both together in heaven.

I remember a couple of months after my father died. The Lord showed me in a vision my father handing out brochures in his old church, Mt. Moriah Baptist. He was so happy and just laughing so much. God showed me that my father had been healed and been made whole. He was in no more pain. Just like the word, says in 2 Corinthians 5:8 NKJV "We are confident, yes, well pleased rather to be absent from the body and to be present with the Lord". My father left this earth with a diseased body. But once he left this earth and became present with the Lord, his diseased body was healed and glorified with the Father.

•

CHAPTER TEN

GUIDANCE

I always had a hunger and thirst for learning the deeper things of God, and I always enjoyed biblical history. I went to seek for a school that would fill the desire I had within me. There was a school called Nyack College in New York I was interested in, but after checking out the curriculum and tuition, I realized this was a school I could not attend at that particular time in my life because the tuition was out of my price range. However, I continued believing that God would open up an opportunity for me.

There was a friend of mine who told me that if it is not available now, put it on a shelf, and it will revisit itself in due season. As time went by, I overheard a conversation from one of the members of Agape Christian Ministries at one of our women functions. It was about a seminary school she was going to. I approached her and asked her about the school and if she could give me some information. The next week I visited the school and I was interested in the classes. Going this route made it more affordable to obtain my degree. I became a student the next semester at Evangelical Bible Institute which was under the umbrella of JD Price Theological Bible College.

Who would have ever thought of me going to seminary school? As I attended the school, I was so intrigued about the classes and teachings that went forth. The professor and other teachers had a way of teaching that kept the classes exciting and they were very knowledgeable.

I remember some of the subjects such as systematic theology, the doctrine of the church, interpreting the scriptures, the foundations of interpretation, introduction to hermeneutics, the prayer of the worshiper — just to name a few of my classes.

Our professor was a walking book of encyclopedias. If anyone still remembers what kind of books these are, they are before the computer ages. My professor had a lot of knowledge and wisdom about the history of religion. We, as a class, became like a family, and we pulled each other through. Before I knew it, I was receiving my associate's degree. I was astonished to complete the classes. There was an inner drive in me to continue and go for my bachelor's degree, and that is what I did. It seemed as though each year, the classes became more and more interesting. I was working a full-time job and coming home doing homework and research papers. It was challenging, but I knew I could only go forward. I said to myself, okay, I am stopping here because I had to really push myself to get to this goal. I remember writing my thesis for my bachelor's degree. It was very demanding. I thought I would never be able to do it because it had been a long time since I was in school, prior to these classes. I remember writing my 25,000-word thesis for my bachelor's degree, and I had to defend my paper. Yet another accomplishment, I finished my bachelor's degree. All I can say is nothing but the Holy Ghost got me through.

As I graduated to receive my bachelor's degree, I remember some of the students asking if I would return for my master's degree. Some of them did, and there was a large part of them that did not. I could understand why not, school was very demanding.

Since, I had such a drive for the word of God and because the dean made it so affordable there was nothing to hold me back. I thought to myself I have to press forward to my higher calling. I enjoyed the classes and I continued to receive my master's degree in

Divinity. Eventually after years of studies, I received my doctorate degree from JD Price Theological Bible College.

Graduation was such a joyous occasion with family and friends. I missed my parents. They would have been so proud of me reaching this milestone. They will forever be in my heart. I was so excited my pastor came from Agape Christian Ministries to put on my tam or Tudor bonnet. I was very emotional. It meant a lot to me that he came. Being a part of a church body is so important in so many ways.

I remember the next semester the dean asked me if I could teach one of the classes. Astonished that he would ask me I was honored to fulfill the task. I prepared myself for the assignment I believed was given to me by God. My first day of teaching was very exciting. I taught Biblical Doctrine, and then the next semester, I taught teaching techniques. The one thing I loved about my walk with God, he prepares you for what is before you. I remember when I was a new believer just coming up in the church. I was asked to teach Sunday school for children five through twelve. At this time, I thought I was not prepared to teach. I remember one of the teachers saying to me that as I teach them, I will also be teaching myself. Here I was now teaching adults at the professor's level. Who would have ever thought? The pain of my past surely became the blueprint for my future.

As the doors opened up for me in school, they also opened up for me at my church Agape Christian Ministries. My pastor asked me to become one of the teachers at the church. We did not have a Sunday school, so we had our Sunday school on Friday nights, and we called it the school of the Bible. At first, I was a little nervous. I remember my pastor telling me, is this not what you went to seminary school for? I said to myself, no, I did not. I only wanted to know a little history about the word of God. But now I know God had a different plan.

As I continued to go through this walk with God, he just kept opening up doors for me. I recall when I was in college the professor taught us how to prepare for a sermon. There were many sermons I did throughout my eight-year period when I was in school. Now was the time for me to practice what I was preaching. My pastor's wife asked me to do a sermon along with two other graduates for the season opener for our Women's Committee. I remember till this day what my sermon was on. It was "You Are Never Alone." The Holy Spirit had His way and the event was very powerful. All I can say is that God is an awesome God!!

CHAPTER ELEVEN

•

NEW BEGINNINGS

Since both of my parents had passed, I thought I had no need to stay in their house any longer. I mentioned to the dean I was not able to teach the next semester. I thank God for opening up that door for me to teach. I do not know what the future holds for me, maybe I will be teaching again.

Dynesha, who had given me problems when she was younger, was now married with her own family and they all are living in South Jersey. She ended up marrying a young man from the high school they both graduated from. There was no one from my family living in my parent's home. The house was now empty, so my brothers and I put the house up for sale. This was hard for me to do since I had lived in the house since I was eight years old. There were a lot of memories there. My prayer was always for someone to move in the house that had a family like my parents had with small children. I thought the school system would be good for young children. It also was convenient to the center of town when they needed things from the stores.

I thought moving closer to my grandchildren would be nice. Every time I would see the family, my grandson would always cry and run away from me, he was at a young age then. He did not know who I was because I did not see him that much. My parent's home was sold to a nice young family and I moved out into an apartment. I said to myself when the time is right, I will then move back to South Jersey. I did not sense the timing was right yet.

In the '90s, when I was going to Word Alive Christian Center, I remember a visiting pastor coming to preach a powerful Word. I can still remember it today. After he ministered the word, he started flowing in the prophetic, and he came to me and said, your house is out there, and your name is on the deed. That was something I always remembered.

Years later, one of the members at the church I was attending Agape Christian Ministries was a real estate agent and a friend of mine. I asked her if I was interested in buying a home in the South Jersey area. Now, a couple of weeks had passed by and she came to me and told me she had some listings and asked if I was interested in looking at any of them. I said, "Of course. Let me know the time and date, and I will meet her at the property."

The next day we met and the first house we went to I was interested in or should I say the model of the townhome. I loved the model home. I was so excited it was just the home I prayed about and everything I wanted. I remember telling the manager at the site which model I was interested in. I filled out all the necessary forms and the rest is history. I could not believe it. I was buying a house that had to be built, from the ground up the way I wanted it to be. We serve an awesome God. It was as if God was orchestrating everything from the beginning to the end. I heard many people say the process of buying a house is very hectic. But I have to say my process went very smoothly because I knew God was in it. This was awesome. Just think of a single parent who once was on welfare, not knowing where her next meal would come from, now I was buying a three-story townhouse by myself with no help from anyone. My name only – a single woman– is on the deed, just like the pastor prophesied over twenty years ago. Well, praise the Lord!!

I was coming into the purpose that God had designed for me. This was the right time to move to South Jersey, and I did. I would miss my Agape family and all that they poured into my life. They will never go unnoticed.

I was living in my brand-new home and enjoying every moment of it. I was living closer to my daughter's family and my grandchildren. My grandson now runs to me when he sees me.

I never had to leave my job when I transitioned because it was in Central Jersey, between North and South Jersey. The trip is a little far, but I thought it would not be long before I retire. I have been working in the health field for forty years now. It was an awesome experience to be able to work in this line of work. It was especially an honor during the COVID-19 pandemic to help in such a critical time when we as a nation were in need.

God is so good. I didn't even have to search for a church home. Because the times I would come to visit Dynesha , I would attend a church called The Family Church in Voorhees, New Jersey under beautiful spiritual leaders. The word was on point and powerful, and their teaching was the same as the other churches I attended.

Just like at Agape Christian Ministries and Word Alive Christian Center these spiritual leaders were approachable and loved the people.

God has been blessing me beyond measure since I moved. God definitely will orchestrate your steps, and yes, all the pain I have gone through, He has walked me into my purpose. I have been awakened from the darkness into His marvelous light.

•

CHAPTER TWELVE

WELL EXPERIENCE

John 4:5–29 NKJV "He came to a city of Samaria which is called Sychar, near the ground that Jacob gave to his son Joseph. Now Jacobs well was there. Jesus, being weary from His journey, sat by the well. A woman from Samaria came to draw water. Jesus said, "Give me a drink." His disciples had gone away into the city to buy food. The woman of Samaria said to Him. "How is it that you, being a Jew ask for a drink from me, a Samaritan?" For Jews have no dealings with Samaritans. Jesus answered and said to her, "If you knew the gift of God and who it is who says to you, give me a drink", you would have asked Him and He would have given you living water." The woman said to Him, Sir, you have nothing to draw with and the well is deep. Where do you get that living water? Are you greater than our father Jacob, who gave us the well and drank from it himself? Jesus answered and said to her, "whoever drinks of this water will thirst again. But whoever drinks the water that I shall give him will never thirst? But the water I shall give him will become in him a fountain of water springing up into everlasting life."

The woman said to Him, Sir, give me this water, that I may not thirst nor come here to draw. Jesus said to her, "Go, call your husband and come here. The woman answered and said I have no husband. Jesus said to her, you have well said I have no husbands for you have had five husbands and the one whom you have now is not your husband, in that you spoke truly. The woman said to

Him. Sir I perceived that you are a prophet. Our fathers worshiped on this mountain, and you Jews say that in Jerusalem is the place where one ought to worship'. Jesus said to her woman believe me, the hour is coming when you will neither on this mountain, nor in Jerusalem, worship the Father. You worship what you do not know, we know what we worship, for salvation is of the Jews. But the hour is coming and now is when the true worshipers will worship in Spirit and truth, for the Father is seeking such to worship Him must worship in spirit and truth. "The woman said to Him," I know that the Messiah is coming. `` When He comes, He will say all things" Jesus said to her, `` I who speak to you is He." The woman then left her waterpot, went her way into the city, and said to the men. Come see a Man who told me all things that I ever did. Could this be Christ? Then they went out of the city and came to Him."

I remember going to a women's conference, and the question was asked, what women in the Bible do you see yourself as? I immediately thought of the Samaritan woman, also known as the woman at the well. My life seemed to exemplify some of the challenges she also went through. Here in this scripture, you will find the Samaritan woman was a woman with no identity. She was only known as the woman at the well. I ask myself why was she not given a name? This could have meant she was a woman of no significance; she had no value or worth. Have you ever felt like you had no significance? Have you ever felt like people just overlook you? Were you ever treated in a way you should not have been? I know there were situations in my life I have.

It is also puzzling to see the Samaritan woman at the well on the hottest time of the day. Many women came to the well later in the cool of the day when it was not so hot. They came to the well in groups not alone like the Samaritan woman did.

In the scripture when Jesus first met with the Samaritan woman at the well the first thing, He ask her was for a drink. She thought it was strange He would ask her since Samaritans did not share things in common with Jews. The good thing here in this story is that Jesus a Jewish man, did talk to her. It is comforting to know that Jesus chooses to love people who believe they are the least to be loved. It does not matter how insignificant you may feel Jesus is there to wrap His arms around you and comfort you in your most challenging time.

The water He was talking about symbolized life or spiritual water and it will turn her whole life around. She would never have to thirst or come back to the well or to the natural water by herself again. The Samaritan woman wanted her life to change for the better so she decided to say yes to Jesus. She wanted the spiritual water to become like a fountain flowing in her belly which would transform her situation. God's Word says it best in John 7:37–38, NKJV"If any thirst let him come to me and drink, he that believes on me out of his belly shall flow rivers of living water."

She was thirsty and this spiritual water quenched or extinguished the thirst she had. When I look in the Merriam Webster dictionary for thirst it is identified as an ardent or a craving or longing for something. The Samaritan woman craved for her situation to be changed by drinking the spiritual water.

What I like about the Samaritan woman was Jesus had given her a chance to choose between the natural water and the spiritual water. We all have chances in life, and we all have consequences to pay, to take the wide road or the narrow road. She chose not to take the natural water but the authentic refreshment of the living water that sprung up everlasting life. When will you come to a point in your life that you know you need Jesus? It's time to stop playing church and be the church. We see here the Samaritan woman continued having a dialogue with Jesus. Do you have a personal relationship with Jesus, whereas he talks to you, and you listen to him and vice versa?

As we continued reading, Jesus said something else to her she would have never imagined. He asked her to call her husband. She responded I have no husband. He said that is so true and the man you are with is not your husband. She probably thought to herself now how did He know that? It seemed she was looking for love in all the wrong places and the wrong spaces to me. It could have been she was looking for someone to complete her because she was not complete within herself. Maybe she also thought things might have been better if she had been married. How many of us believe maybe if I marry him, he will love me more? We think all kinds of crazy things when we think we can draw someone closer to us. She could have been a needy woman or one who had low self–esteem or just wandering we do not know. You must ask yourself one thing, and I know this too well because I did it also. Are you replacing relationships with men, and I mean those men not worthy of your time, before God? Are you like the Samaritan woman you keep going around and around the same old mountain with the same kind of men getting the same old results? Looking for a void that only God can fill? If she would have just looked deeper within herself she would have known it was not in the men, it is in Jesus she will find happiness. It took the Samaritan woman five times to be married to figure it out, and she was still wrong. The sixth man who came into her life was still not her husband. It was not until the seventh man who is Jesus came into her life to complete her. She realized at this time He was the prophet.

She also realized that her fore–fathers worshiped on this very mountain. It was the Jews who sought that in Jerusalem this was the place where one ought to worship. But God was about to introduce her to a new form of worship, one that was of spirit and truth.

God has given us a way to which His presence can be accessed and this way is praise and worship. Worship is the destination that God desires us to reach, and praise is the vehicle we use to get there. God desires that we come into His presence.

When we say we must worship in "spirit" it must originate from within, from our heart; it must be sincere by our love for God and gratitude for all He is and has done. Worship can't be mechanical or formalistic. It says in Philippians 3:3 NKJV "for we are circumcised, who worship God in the Spirit, rejoice in Christ Jesus and have no confidence in the flesh."

It is not what we do with our hands (or don't do) with our hands (or what someone else is doing or not doing), but what we do with our hearts and minds– because of the one who has captured our hearts and minds. We must always remember God is Spirit and those who worship Him must worship in spirit and in truth.

When the Samaritan woman found out the man at the well was the Messiah, she dropped her jar. She ran to tell everyone in the city who this man was who knew all about her past. Would it be a beautiful thing if we dropped the things that hinder us from reaching Jesus? Do you still see yourself in the story? I sure do. When we run into obstacles in our life, we feel we can fix it on our own, and we do not need God. We are empty inside, searching and longing and reaching for things that only God can give us.

Many people are waiting for you to go and run and tell those in the city what God did in your life. We all have testimonies of our own that we can share and tell others about the goodness of God. Just think of the woman who is being abused and nowhere for her or her children to go. She needs to hear from someone like you to tell her I was in your same predicament and this is what God did for me. Let them know He can do the same for them.

The woman who goes to the doctor then finds out she has cancer and she has no help at home. I work with patients who have been diagnosed with cancer every day. Just imagine if I did not open up my compassion to console them at their most challenging time. There are many situations and trials that we go through whereas we can help someone who is going through what we might have already triumphed over. People need the Jesus kind of love that we could portray to them. I believe each and every one of us God has assigned someone for us to speak life into.

CHAPTER THIRTEEN

•

AWAKENING

It was a long journey for me to get to this point in my life. I now realized I was God's masterpiece. When I look back over my life, God did not see all the wrong I saw in myself. He said I am not a mistake; I was planned and handcrafted by him. I am one-of-a-kind an original. I am a masterpiece in every sense of the way.

Paul says it well in Ephesians 2:1-10 "NKJV "You he made alive who were dead in trespasses and sins, and which you once walked according to the course of this world according to the prince of the power of this world, according to the prince of the power of the air, the spirit who now works in the sons of disobedience, among whom also we once conducted ourselves in the loss of our flesh fulfilling the desires of the flesh and of the mind, and we're up by nature of wrath, just as the others. But God who is rich in mercy, because of his great love with which he loved, even when we were dead in trespasses, made us alive together with Christ and raised us up together and made us sit together in the heavenly places in Christ Jesus, that in the ages to come, He might show the exceeding riches of his grace and his kindness towards Christ Jesus. For by grace, you have been saved through faith and not of yourselves. It is the gift of God, not of works lest anyone should boast. For we are his masterpiece created in Christ Jesus for good works which God prepared beforehand that we should walk in them."

My spirit awakened from the empty places to the things of God. All the old ways of thinking started to die, and everything started to become new in my life. The more my life started to change, the freer I became in my mind, the freer I became in my body, and my soul became free. The Lord is the Spirit, and where the spirit of the Lord is, there is liberty.

We have to look at ourselves beyond our pain. The testimonies I have shared in the past pages are not to just tell you all my business but to show you what an awesome God we serve. It does not matter what your backdrop looks like; God is there with you. The woman at the well and her past challenges, a woman who was not even worthy of having a name, she ran into Jesus, and He turned her whole life around. You may have come from the streets on drugs. You may be laying and playing like I did. I am telling you there is a God who loves deeper than you will ever know. He will show you unconditional love. He will quench a thirst you have been searching for all your life. It doesn't matter where you have come from. God is right there with you.

In God's word, you see many people whose life did not seem to match up. David had lustful desires for another man's wife and ended up being Jesus' mighty man of valor, a man after God's own heart. Jonah was a bigot; he ran from God and was swallowed up by a fish. He ended up preaching power to the people to repent. There are so many people in the Bible who did not exemplify a life of righteousness.

God has a plan for you. He wants your inconsistencies, and all those things that you sensed are imperfect, he can use them for His glory.

There is a side to the trials and tribulations of life that we go through that we miss. We are not to focus on the pain but the greater purpose that will come out of all it. If you can see the purpose behind the pain, we can find our way out of the lie. If you can see the purpose beyond the pain, you will understand

God's ability to leverage the suffering in your life for a greater cause. Only when we give our situation to God can He purify our motives and teach us wonderful things. We can only learn when our suffering humbles us. Then He forces us to pay attention to the deep work the Holy Spirit is doing within you. God is not out there to hurt us, as so many may say. The world we live in hurts us. People hurt each other. Greed, violence, war, and deception are everywhere. There are cycles of sickness, poverty, and death. God did not create these things to hurt us. He is the one who wants to help the broken people.

God did not orchestrate purposeless suffering, but he redeems us from our suffering as a witness of His glory. He shows others through our sufferings how as they seek His face, they, too, can be healed and set free.

I would like to speak to the women who may have been molested, abused, and misused. There is a greater calling on your life. It does not matter what your situation is. God loves you. You do not have to be like me or the woman at the well trying to find love in other men. A love that they could never quench. Unconditional love that has no limits is a love that will flow like rivers of living water. Accept him into your heart and believe and trust Him. Trust that the plan he has for you shall be established. You can see in my journey how God sent people into my life, but He also removed people from my life. He is the one who does the putting together and the taking apart.

Here I can say as I stood on the word of God, he has done some miraculous things in my life, and it is all because I surrendered it all. I lived a lifestyle that could have led to destruction, but because of His love, I went down a different path. I thank God for the roads I traveled because I would not be the person I am today if I had not.

Again, just like the woman at the well, when Jesus was able to call her up on all her past lifestyle choices, she realized that He was her Messiah. She dropped her jar, the very jar she was to use for her natural thirst, and she ran into the city to tell everyone about this man named Jesus.

I, too, have dropped my jar like the woman at the well. I say to you what is your jar for you to let go? It could be anything from drugs, alcohol, pride, promiscuity and greed. You fill in the slot. Seek God and He will reveal it to you.

I will run to tell the many women that God sends my way about a man named Jesus. I will tell them how God can fulfill their natural thirst for the spiritual water and they will never thirst again.

•

CHAPTER FOURTEEN

UNDERSTANDING YOUR PURPOSE

As I backtrack the years of my trials, and tribulations, I've come to understand my purpose. I did not understand it when I was going through it all. But as God walked me through and awakened me through the challenges, I could see my purpose so much clearer.

I understand how the discovery of purpose is actually awakening to what has always been in my life. There is something we all have been searching for, and that something has been with us all along. In God's word, he says he knows our end in the beginning. Jeremiah 1:5 NJKV says, "before I formed you in the womb, I knew you." He knows what we would be like before we were born; it says He knew us. If he knew us, then I believe He knows where we are going to be. He knows the challenges we will go through before we go through them. He is right there to guide us in the way He wants us to go. Psalm 139:1-4 (NKJV) says, "Oh, Lord, you have searched me and known me. You know my sitting down and my rising up, you understand my thoughts afar off. You comprehend my path and my lying down. And are acquainted with all my ways."

When it comes to our purpose and awakening, God knows everything about us. He knows who our parents will be, and he knows how our lifestyle will be. Just think, it was all planned from the beginning. He uses the good, the bad, and the ugly parts of our lives to create someone beautiful in His eyes. His Word in Romans

8:28 NKJV" says and we know all things work together for good to those who love God to those who are called according to His purpose"

We must understand there is nothing we have to regret about yesterday. Our purpose can't happen too soon or too late; everything has its own timing. Sometimes there are things in our lives we are just not ready for, and if we do them prematurely, we might just mess them up. As you heard in my story, God prepared me for teaching long before I received my doctorate degree. But after I went through the process step by step, he said, "Now you are ready. I believe teaching was in me before I was born in my mother's womb. If you look deep within you will find that little boy or girl in you.

Each and every one of us has dreams, talents, and aspirations lying dormant within us. It is only when you have become awakened to the things of God they are birthed into your purpose.

Everything in life evolves. Evolution is about the progressive unfolding of a thing. Or, as the Merriam–Webster dictionary puts it — a process of continuous change from a lower to a higher, more complex, or better state or growth.

I heard a Pastor preach this on a Sunday," evolution happens when time and space catch up to what the eternal realm has already experienced."

Our lives have already been carried out and perfected in the eternal realm. It is something that has to be worked out, but what's been lived out has already been established. It is mind–blowing when you start to search for the deeper things of God. Purpose is not something that is revealed to you once, and you are set for life. Your purpose must continue to evolve with your life until your life resembles what God foreknew about you.

We must know that purpose is not an activity, destination, or location. Your purpose is awareness. No matter where you are in life, you have to keep going and pursuing God's will. The awareness of purpose says I have not arrived yet and must remain open to the next instruction until every detail of God's plan for me has been accomplished.

I can remember my walk with the Lord when I was a member of Word Alive Christian Center. The women's ministry had a course some of the women of the body were a part of. The course was called purity with a purpose. As mentioned earlier in my journey, I remember the course had a strict curriculum, and many women were delivered from many hurts and pains in that course, including myself. But one thing I took away from the course was this one scripture –Philippians 3:12, "NJKVNot that I already attained, or am already perfected, but I press on that I may lay hold of that for which Christ Jesus has also laid hold of me." When I look at this scripture, even at that time in my life when the struggle was real, I knew that purpose had taken hold of me for something, but I had not fully grasped all that it was. I had been walking with God on purpose, and I was accomplishing a lot, but I knew there was so much more of me to come. I was going to continue holding on and pushing through. But what I was not going to do was get stuck in the last place my purpose had taken me. My purpose was evolving, and I was to stay on the course that God was taking me.

I am understanding now that my purpose is the life that God has designed for me. You are living out the reason that God brought you into this world. As God guides you and directs you in the way He wants you to go, you are walking into your purpose. You must hear the voice of God but not only hear his voice, you must be obedient to do what He says. The one who does the guiding is the Holy Spirit as in John 14:26, "AMP He is our helper, counselor, intercessor, advocate, strengthener and so much more. The Holy Spirit whom the Father will send in my name (in my place, to represent me and act on my behalf), he will teach you all things. He will cause you to recall everything I have told you".

The Holy Spirit knows everything there is to know about your life because He knows our end in the beginning. He knows how to get us exactly where He wants us to go. He knows your journey, and when you make a mistake along the path, He knows how to put you back on purpose. It is something like your GPS on your car. When you are going the wrong way, it will reroute you to show you how to go the right way.

As you have a relationship with the Holy Spirit, as you are talking with Him, He is talking back with you. Let me tell you how awesome the Holy Spirit is. It was the relationship I was in with Ray that seemed to be disturbing to me. From the beginning of the relationship, there was a grieving or distress in my spirit only when I was around him. I could not put my finger on exactly what it meant, but it seemed like something was not right. Then it went from the grievance to the Holy Spirit speaking to me, telling me that Ray was a counterfeit. He was not the kind of person that he was trying to portray. Because I had a relationship with the Holy Spirit at this time, I knew now what the Holy Spirit was saying. Ray was everything I ever wanted in a man. The Holy Spirit was telling me to get out of the relationship because that was not the man He had for me. But to me, he looked like him, smelled like him, and everything about him to me shouted he was to be my future husband. After spending time with Ray, yes, he began to show me who he really was. Just like the Holy Spirit warned me, he turned out to be something he really was not. After I ended the relationship, the grievances went away. If I had not had a relationship and received the warning from the Holy Spirit, I might have gone down a road of pain and heartache. If I knew this earlier in my journey, I would not have gone through all the disappointments that I did. But then again everything is in God's timing, I had to learn something through my heartaches.

One thing to know about the Holy Spirit is his only objective is to prosper you on your path to purpose. When you follow His lead and move in the right direction, He is pleased, and you can sense it within.

As I continue on my road to purpose, everything begins to feel right. Everything seems to be going in the right direction, even how I am writing this book. It was a divine setup from God. It was spoken in my life years ago, around 1995, that I would be writing about relationships in the body of Christ. At that point in my life, I said no way it could have happened. It was at that time I was in a very dark season. As I mentioned earlier, everything has the right timing for it to be manifested. As God molded me and continues to shape me, I am coming into what He wants me to be. I am learning how to press towards those things that He wants me to do for Him. This is what purpose does when you begin on this path. It cultivates the things needed to bring you to the place that allows your purpose to be fulfilled.

As we continue on the road, we make mistakes along the journey because I know I have. The marvelous thing about God is it does not matter what we have been through. He is there to wipe us off and make us anew.

We can relate it to the caterpillar that turns into a beautiful butterfly. When a caterpillar undergoes a metamorphosis, it does it inside a pointed bean-shaped enclosure called the cocoon. In this process, the caterpillar falls apart completely, it separates, disintegrates or loses all shape of consciousness. Literally, the caterpillar dies to become a butterfly. This is called the chrysalis process.

Just like the caterpillar, we must die to ourselves, and we must die to things of the world. We must transform our way of thinking, renew our minds, and accept Jesus into our lives. He will begin the process in you as you go through your chrysalis process like the caterpillar, and He will make you anew, like the butterfly. You will see old things will pass away, and all things will become new in your life. You will be on your way to the purpose that God has ordained for you since the beginning of time.

Purpose finds you at the right time. It is a timing thing. When you look in Ecclesiastes 3:1 NKJVsays, "to everything, there is a season, a time for every purpose under heaven.".

I know my life purpose is to become the woman of strength, the woman of dignity, the woman of grace, the woman of purpose, the woman of integrity, the woman of hope, and the woman of wisdom. I want to be an example of one who builds her foundation on Jesus Christ so that others may follow me as I follow Christ, and to continue to walk in integrity and in intimacy with Jesus Christ all the days of my life.

•

CHAPTER FIFTEEN

ENOUGH SAID

I remember the Lord speaking these words a while back, and it resonated with me, and I would like to share it with you. It is words that can be spoken to any one of us. Listen to your heart and listen to what God is saying to you through these words.

"Listen to your Spirit or Listen to your Soul."

Enough Said

Who do you say that I am? When you listen to your Spirit, it shouts your name real loud. Put your name here ————. Who do you say that I am? Because I know who I say that you are.

You are beautifully and wonderfully made. You are the apple of my eye. I know your comings, and I know your goings. There is nowhere you can hide from me. I will be with you till the end of time. I will never leave you nor forsake you. When all others have left you, I am still there with you. My child, when you listen to your Spirit, you shall hear me, my voice in the inner depth of your soul.

But you are too busy to hear. In your coming and going, in your doing for everyone but me, you can't hear me. For I try to get your attention, but you will not hear me.

I was there when you were having trouble on your job, but you did not hear me. I was there when you were having trouble with your child, but you did not hear me. Whatever trial that came your way, I was there, but you did not hear me. You see, you got caught up in the circumstances and let it control you instead of getting caught up in me and letting me lead you. So, who do you say that I am? Do you hear me with your Spirit man, or do you hear me in your soul? Do you get caught up in the things that I bless you with, or do you get to know who I am ? I believe it is a blessing. Yes, you get caught up in my blessings. You get caught up in the big house. Yes, you get caught up in the expensive car. Yes, you get caught up in the name doctor, lawyer, deacon, minister, evangelist etc., but do you ever search the things of the Spirit? Do you know how much I love you? Do you know how much I care about you? I know every strand of hair on your head and every strand you've lost. Do you know how much I care about your lost soul? If you asked me, I would be there for you. I will guide you and direct you in the way you should go. Wait for me and do not lean unto your own understanding but trust in me only. For I will not lead you wrong like others you put your trust in. Take time to listen to my voice in the middle of the night. When I wake you at 2:00 a.m., I want to have a conversation with you. I want some alone time. But instead, you turn on the television and block me out.

Enough said! Do you know me at all, or do you want to even get to know me? How about this, let me take away the things that you enjoy in life. Let me take away the things you take for granted, like the very breath that you breathe every minute, every second, then will you hear me in the middle of the night? Listen to your Spirit, my child or listen to your soul.

I have created you and designed you to multiply. I have created you to spread the gospel of my Word. How can you do this when you do not know who you are? For you are lost, even yourself, so who will spread my word in such a lost world? I need you, and you need me. I need you to be obedient to my word. Live by my word and listen to my word. You need me in every situation of your life. So now, who do you think that I am? Yes, I am your lifeline. There is nothing that you can do without me. Listen to your Spirit or listen to your Soul? Enough Said!

I wanted to share this because God was trying to get my attention at this point in my life. I seemed to have time to accomplish everything else in my life except spending time with God. He said He will wake me up in the middle of the night, but I will not adhere to the call. Instead of listening to His voice yet again, I would turn on the TV, which is the distraction.

I remember the story about Martha and Mary. They were sisters of Lazarus, the man that Jesus raised from the dead. One day Jesus and His disciples stopped to visit their home. Mary was sitting at the feet of Jesus, listening intently to his words. Meanwhile, Martha was distracted, working frantically, preparing and serving the guests. Martha did not like the fact that Mary was sitting at Jesus' feet and she was busy preparing for the guest. Her question to Jesus was He did not care about her.

Jesus said Luke10: 41-41 NKJV "Martha, Martha, the Lord answered, you are worried and upset about many things, but few things are needed or indeed only one. Mary has chosen what is better, and it will not be taken away from her."

Just like in this story, we should make Jesus our priority in our lives, not that it is wrong to help with the normal affairs of your life. Sitting at the feet of Jesus is best. Good works should flow from a Christ-centered life, but when we give him the attention he deserves, he empowers us.

Made in the USA
Middletown, DE
13 September 2024

60313607R00070